Pentecostalism
in America

Pentecostalism in America

R. G. ROBINS

 PRAEGER

AN IMPRINT OF ABC-CLIO, LLC
Santa Barbara, California • Denver, Colorado • Oxford, England

Library of Congress Cataloging-in-Publication Data

Robins, R. G.
   Pentecostalism in America / R. G. Robins.
      p. cm.
   Includes bibliographical references (p.) and index.
      ISBN 978-0-313-35294-2 (hard copy : alk. paper) — ISBN 978-0-313-35295-9 (ebook)
   1. Pentecostalism—United States—History.   2. United States—Church history.   I. Title.
   BR1644.5.U6R63   2010
   277.3'082—dc22   2010017626

ISBN: 978-0-313-35294-2
EISBN: 978-0-313-35295-9

14   13   12   11   10   1   2   3   4   5

This book is also available on the World Wide Web as an eBook.
Visit www.abc-clio.com for details.

Praeger
An Imprint of ABC-CLIO, LLC

ABC-CLIO, LLC
130 Cremona Drive, P.O. Box 1911
Santa Barbara, California 93116-1911

This book is printed on acid-free paper

Manufactured in the United States of America

To Yoko Asano Robins
You have made these the best years of my life.

Contents

Introduction   ix

1   The Origins of American Pentecostalism   1

2   A New Religion for a New Millennium   21

3   Pentecost and the World at War   49

4   America's Pentecost   73

5   A Mighty Host   105

Conclusion   141

Bibliography   149

Index   153

Introduction

Most of what a historian writes, I've heard it said, is autobiographical. In this case at least, the adage is true, and readers might be edified or perhaps forewarned by a brief accounting of the fact. I'm an ex-holy roller and I make no bones about it.

I literally cut my teeth on the pews of the First Pentecostal Church of God of Union Bower, Texas, where my father had been installed as pastor two years before I was born, and where he remained for the rest of his working life; my earliest memories include the savory sensation of biting through the bittersweet skin of varnish on our rounded pew tops to hit solid wood beneath. Union Bower—in the days before Irving, made ravenous by suburbanization, swallowed it up—was a hardscrabble neighborhood where dogs ran free and the Johnson grass went uncut. If there had been railroad tracks in our vicinity, Union Bower would have been on the wrong side of them.

I have many recollections of what became Irving First, but all of them are enveloped in something deeper still: a remembered atmosphere of humid air stirred by pulsing music loud enough to feel, an invisible blanket of liquid decibels. Growing up Pentecostal then was not like it is now. Well into the 1960s, the Pentecostal Church of God resisted the acculturation that I describe in the book, and ours was a "shouting" church, a tightly boundaried community that carried its ecstasies deep into the night.

At its heyday, Irving First fielded a high-powered band with piano and organ, bass and electric guitar, drum and tambourine, and whatever other stray instrument someone might bring along on a given night. When the song leader, Brother Crisp, cut loose a honky-tonk rendition of, say, "Jesus on the Mainline," the entire congregation was liable to erupt in a flush of shoutin', dancin', Jerico-marchin' Holy Ghost delirium that would bring the house down. It was no place for the faint of heart.

But it was a fine place for children. While the sacred tumult raged, kids roamed free. As a toddler I would slip quietly into that narrow realm beneath the pews, lie flat against the cool tile, and play while the great, strident world of adults carried on above. I had the place to myself, usually, though it was always possible for an adult to hit the floor and come rolling through. As children, time was on our side. Services ran late, and even when the strenuous ecstasies subsided, our parents would pool like actors backstage after a performance—a giddy, neurochemical flow fueling conversation long after.

Church was life, but we never failed to give formal education its rightful place. Which was at the back of the line. As that sentence fragment illustrates. The ancient tradition of East Texas Pentecostal protocol decreed that services should be held Wednesday night, Friday night, and twice on Sundays, with the first Monday of each month set aside for fellowship meeting and youth rally. That schedule left ample time for occasional revivals, which ran nightly for anywhere from one to four weeks straight. With a round or two of street witnessing thrown into the mix, book learning had to fend for itself. Church ruled, and school drooled.

School was also painful, a world of generalized angst punctuated by acute dilemmas. There we met the "other" and came to know the stigma it imprinted on us and the consternation we inflicted on it. This encounter was especially hard on my sisters, forbidden to wear makeup or cut their hair and forced to wear long skirts while everyone else caught a whiff of the Sixties. But it was no picnic for my brother and me, either. In those days, dancing was a formidable sin, and I spent one year caught in the crossfire between my parents and a well-meaning teacher who vainly hoped to liberate me from their rigid strictures by forcing me to sashay and do-si-do in her square-dancing class. Experiences of the sort left me with a convoluted sense of inferiority and divine election that, through several permutations, still yields its wounded consolations.

It stands to reason that a good profiler could draw up a compendium of traits shared by a high percentage of natural-born Pentecostals of my generation. The list would surely include an instinct to go against the grain; a romantic urge to follow one's heart; a delight in spontaneity with its corresponding aversion to the script; and, of course, a baneful taste for peak experiences. Buried somewhere amid the ingrained reflexes that sustain and bedevil us ex-holy rollers, moreover, would be one of particular advantage to the scholar. The experience in one's formative years of watching grown-ups publicly scream, weep, run, leap, thrash, flail, fall prostrate, speak in tongues, and generally cavort about—and the experience of joining right in as one comes of age—tends to broaden one's perception of the normal. The ex-holy roller, that is to say, makes a natural social scientist. Or, absent the benefit of higher education, a likely guest for Jerry Springer. I feel fortunate to have inherited this mélange of traits, each with its toothy charm and its unsavory consequences, except on those occasions when I don't.

Somewhere over the course of years I drifted to the outer limits of my native world and then, whether by force of happenstance, deep thinking, or acute indigestion, popped through to the other side. Like exes of many different kinds, I found myself disoriented, self-estranged, peering back in befuddlement at my own nurturing matrix as if into an inscrutable, translucent crystal ball. A single question formed itself in my mind: "What was *that*?"

So let me confess. I have a conflicted relationship with my Pentecostal past. Sometimes, I look at myself and my siblings with all of our quirks, flaws, and sundry disorders, and I'm tempted to blame our religion. But then again, I know that's only half a truth, because there are those other times, like when I straggle into an uptown high church and watch milquetoast frissons ripple through the congregants as their choir downshifts into some honkified spiritual, and I think back to Brother Elmer shouting like a turbo-charged whirling dervish and Sister Trixie, head snapping like a whip, unleashing a staccato stream of other tongues while Sister Vivien torched the piano and Brother Cooper, on the nights he wasn't backslidden, flayed the drums and while my own preacher-man daddy split nifty rifts off his Gretch Signature guitar, with Sister Shirley all the while belting out the gospel blues like some soulful Holy Ghost Loretta Lynn, and, well, I think of that and then I know what *that* was and it was old-time Pentecost and it could make a tired old sinner want to get up and shout. Wounded? Maybe. But a damned good consolation.

This book, then, like my first, is a by-product of my attempt to come to terms with growing up Pentecostal.

In the chapters ahead, I have tried to give narrative form to the broad historical sweep of American Pentecostalism. With a movement of such scale and complexity, however, the narrative threads must be as few as they are resilient. Primarily, this is a story about organic growth and evolution. I adhere to a chronological framework, noting the shifting contours and character of Pentecostalism, its major figures and factions, as the movement changes and ramifies over time. The overarching themes concern Pentecostalism's fraught pilgrimage into the evangelical wing of the American mainstream and the movement's irrepressible adaptability. But even these motifs must be spun lightly, since they do not apply equally to all parts of the movement. Along the way, I trust that the sinews binding this sprawling phenomenon into a single movement will become clear: a common past, distinctive practices, a core of shared assumptions, and a gripping certainty that every living day gleams as resplendent with power and promise as those recorded in the pages of Holy Scripture.

Chapter one traces the 19th-century roots of American Pentecostalism, surveying the growth and radicalization of the Holiness movement and introducing the individuals, ideas, and networks that would ultimately create and define Pentecostalism. The chapter spans from the mid-1800s to the beginning of the 20th century.

Chapter two describes the birth of Pentecostalism, introducing its leading personalities and analyzing its culture, beliefs, and spirituality. The chapter also sketches the movement's early networks and discusses the major controversies that fractured the movement in the 1910s. Finally, it treats the rise of Pentecostal denominations. Chronologically, it takes us from the beginning of the 20th century to the brink of the First World War.

Chapter three looks at Pentecostalism between the great wars, with particular attention to changes in the movement's religious culture and the rising strength and professionalism of its major institutions. It addresses the movement's evolving attitudes toward war and nation and charts its early steps toward broader social engagement.

Chapter four follows American Pentecostalism from the end of the Second World War to the early 1970s, a period when demographic growth and rising institutional strength carried the movement to new heights of influence. It describes the assimilation of many Pentecostals into the broader world of evangelicalism and looks at revitalizing countercurrents like the great midcentury deliverance revivals. In addition, it covers the rise of the charismatic movement and looks at areas of dynamic convergence that increasingly defied traditional labels, such as the Jesus People movement.

Chapter five brings us from the early 1970s to the present. It surveys Pentecostalism's continued assimilation and pays in-depth attention to the recent politicization of the movement. The chapter also analyzes dynamic zones of convergence where Pentecostalism, evangelicalism, and the charismatic movement meet and overlap, touching on revitalization movements, televangelism, the Positive Confession movement, and the megachurch phenomenon. In addition, it discusses the increasing diversity and global character of Pentecostalism.

Finally, a short conclusion presents issues and challenges facing Pentecostalism as it moves further into the 21st century, and also provides a table of selected Pentecostal denominations.

I have not attempted to assess Pentecostalism in any normative way. Rather, my goal throughout has been to describe and explain the movement, to place it in historical context, and in this way to render it knowable and its appeal comprehensible to outsiders looking in. I do hope, however, that I have paid some tribute to the generous, passionate hearts of the wonderful Pentecostal people who fashioned the world of my youth and who gave me more of life than I can ever repay.

Many individuals have lent support and encouragement to me along the way. When an unexpected turn of events seemed to place the project in jeopardy, Dr. David Satterwhite and Mizuho Iwata of Fulbright Japan came to my aid and encouraged me to press on, as did my wonderful colleagues at Tokyo University. At the most critical phase of the book's composition, I relied on the library services of Bethel College of Mishawaka, Indiana, and Notre Dame University of South Bend, Indiana, to whom I now express my thanks. As with everything I have done or will do professionally, I acknowledge my debt to Grant Wacker, who read the manuscript and did his best to limit its defects. His scholarship has set a standard of wisdom, wit, and grace that historians of Pentecostal origin ever after will aim for and fall short of. With every passing year, I better understand the enduring importance of family. I want to thank my parents, my siblings, my children, and above all my enchanting wife Yoko, to whom this book is dedicated.

And one last thing. I know it comes a few decades late and this may not be the best place for it, but I would like to apologize to our old non-Pentecostal neighbors, who endured countless nights of what must have seemed an unconscionable racket. I sincerely regret the trouble we caused you. But we had Jesus on the mainline, and had to tell him what we want.

Roger Robins

CHAPTER 1

The Origins of American Pentecostalism

In the course of little more than a century, American Pentecostalism has expanded into a movement of striking range and diversity. Setting aside its many global incarnations, Pentecostalism in the United States alone nearly defies categorization. It is the megachurch and the storefront mission, the tent meeting and the support group, the affluent suburb and the rural hamlet and the hard-pressed inner-city street. It comes in dozens of ethnic varieties and encompasses theological divisions that touch issues as basic as the nature of God, the way of full salvation, the correct form of church government, and the proper Christian stance toward the world and its political regimes. Indeed, viewed solely in terms of its current manifestations, one wonders how it can be treated as a single movement at all.

Our survey of American Pentecostalism will in fact reveal elements of a shared religious culture, but the true unity amid this plenitude of forms lies in an organic relation to a common past. The story of American Pentecostalism is the story of an extended family, one continuously reshaped by additions and departures and mergers but bound by its origins in a particular set of historical events. Our journey toward an understanding of the present, then, begins in the past, with the story behind our story.

HOLINESS

Pentecostalism sprang from a post–Civil War irruption of heroic Christianity known to historians as the American Holiness movement.

Holiness had been a growing evangelical preoccupation since the rediscovery (and redefinition) of John Wesley's doctrine of "entire sanctification" during the period of early 19th-century revivalism known as the Second Great Awakening. Methodists like Timothy Merritt and Phoebe Palmer taught that entire sanctification constituted a definite experience subsequent to conversion that shattered the hold of sin and thus enabled Christians to reach a state of Perfect Love. Evangelical currents had long been carrying the nation's religious culture in a direction uniquely favorable to Methodism, with its democratic spirit, its pietistic fervor, and its ecumenical emphasis on ethics and experience over doctrines or creeds—and here again a Wesleyan theme took hold. The pursuit of this "second blessing" recast the ancient ascetic merger of intense emotion with severe ethics and inspired a movement for "Christian perfection" that soon overflowed its Wesleyan banks, being modified and diffused by non-Methodists as diverse as the Presbyterians Charles Finney, Asa Mahan, and William Boardman and the Congregationalist Thomas Upham.

Holiness in that guise proved vital to the perfectionist mood and reforming zeal of antebellum America, but its full flowering only emerged in the years following the Civil War. There it exfoliated into a broad, dynamic, and controversial coalition of emphases—a religious gestalt, really—that formed the matrix of American Pentecostalism. By the last quarter of the 19th century, that is to say, the Holiness movement had come to mean much more than just holiness.

By any measure, the half-century following America's devastating civil war stands out for its transformational character. Even as the pall of more than 600,000 deaths still cast its shadow, a complex web of interlocking systems of labor, industry, engineering, finance, transportation, communication, and politics burgeoned into an integrated social order that, for the first time, physically resembled our own. Between 1860 and 1910, the nation's population tripled, from just over 31 million to 92 million, and 23 million immigrants joined rural migrants pressing into the swelling cities, farmlands, and mining towns of America. Most found the pace exhilarating, attended as it was by a stream of technological wonderments conjured by scientific invention, but the transformation also brought squalor on a heretofore unimagined scale, new forms of rootlessness, and disillusion regarding the ability of established institutions to solve the problems of modern life. Social conflicts pitted immigrants against Old-Stock Americans, Catholics against Protestants, labor against capital. The American South, though scarcely touched by immigration, saw postwar Reconstruction collapse into a segregated order whose racial lines were maintained by instruments of terror. In every region, Americans born in the 1820s and 1830s grew old in a world that could not have been imagined in their youth.

Evangelical Christians rushed to meet the needs and seize the opportunities of the conflicted age, and, within that social-religious crucible, sanctification catalyzed with other powerful themes to create a new Holiness movement.

The movement's driving force in the immediate postwar years remained Wesleyan, but of a yet more diverse and ecumenical sort. To begin with, the Methodist Church itself had been fractured by the trauma of abolition and war. Two small Holiness bodies—the Wesleyan Methodist Church and the Free Methodist Church—had broken away in 1843 and 1860, respectively, and the main denomination had divided into northern and southern wings in 1844. In an effort perhaps to heal their own ecclesiastical wounds as much as those of a severed nation, an influential group of Holiness Methodists led by John Inskip, Matthew Simpson, and William Osborn looked to a time-honored medium, the camp meeting, to dispense the remedy of Christian Perfection. An 1867 camp meeting at Vineland, New Jersey, led to the organization of the National Camp Meeting Association for the Promotion of Christian Holiness in 1868. With Inskip at its helm, the National Campmeeting Association encouraged the formation of state and local Holiness associations and began publishing a periodical, the *Christian Witness and Advocate of Bible Holiness*, which carried its influence further still.

Holiness camp meetings met enormous success. As the embodiment of old-time religion, they provided a link to an integrated past. Within the embracing boundaries of the camp, washed in the blood of Christ and the zeal of Christian perfection, men and women relived a world whose harmony had not been shattered by social enmity, and so found means to reform their present world. Local and regional camp meetings and associations proliferated, and general Holiness conventions soon emerged.

Ecumenicity had always been a feature of American Holiness. Now it became a defining trait. As America's main conduit for European pietism—a "religion of the heart" that responded to war and creedal division in Christendom by appealing to the perceived common ground of spiritual experience and practical ethics—Methodists were the masters of fraternal overture. Heaven held no Episcopalians, Presbyterians, Independents, or Methodists, George Whitefield had intoned, only Christians, and Wesley had adopted Augustine's irenic formula: "in essentials unity, in non-essentials liberty, and in all things charity." Soon, however, some Methodist bishops began to fret that the Holiness movement had little but liberty and charity.

The movement's success ultimately doomed its relationship with Methodist authorities. Local, state, and regional associations proliferated, often with their own camp meetings, evangelists, and publications. By the 1880s, an increasing number were either formally or effectively independent, and their memberships drew on the full panoply of America's evangelical denominations. The Methodist-inspired camp meeting associations, then, spread the good news of entire sanctification with great efficiency, but they did so within an intensely syncretistic milieu that encouraged cross-pollination, especially among the more radical elements of American evangelicalism.

HOLY GHOST BAPTISM

Nowhere was that cross-pollination more apparent than with respect to a parallel current that ran alongside of and increasingly merged into the Wesleyan Holiness movement. As the 19th century progressed, fascination with the person and work of the Holy Spirit flourished in American Protestantism, liberal and conservative alike. That fascination worked with particular effect on non-Wesleyan advocates of Christian perfection whose Presbyterian, Congregational, Baptist, or Anglican affiliations linked them to midcentury "Reformed" Holiness figures like Finney and Mahan. Though often influenced by Methodists, they spoke less of entire sanctification than of what Boardman had called "the higher Christian life," and since the time of Mahan, they had equated this experience with the "Baptism with the Holy Ghost" that had empowered the disciples on the Day of Pentecost.

By the late 1880s, a new generation of gifted leaders had come to the fore. It included Adoniram Judson Gordon, Baptist pastor of Boston's Clarendon Street Church; Dwight Lyman Moody, heir to Finney as the most famous evangelist of his day; Presbyterian pastor and writer Arthur Tappan Pierson; Congregational theologian Reuben Archer Torrey; and Albert Benjamin Simpson, founder of what became the Christian and Missionary Alliance. Like their Wesleyan Holiness allies, this wing of the movement had its own institutional structures, which included missionary training schools in Boston, Chicago, and Nyack, New York; Moody's Northfield conferences; and an important conference center at Keswick, England.

Many in the Higher Life wing of the Holiness movement did not agree that sanctification eradicated the sinful nature and preferred to think of Baptism with the Holy Ghost in terms of power for service rather than cleansing from sin. But for much of the rank and file, this was a distinction without a difference. All Holiness saints wanted both, and Higher Life saints frequently did anticipate Wesleyan-style sanctification. Indeed, the Keswick conference had been founded by the Quaker-turned-Methodist couple Hannah Whitall Smith and Robert Pearsall Smith, with assistance from Boardman, whose views on and experience of sanctification were much indebted to Phoebe Palmer. But regardless of how one parsed the experience of sanctification, by the post–Civil War period, Wesleyan and Reformed advocates alike coveted power and purification, and both camps sought Holy Ghost baptism as a second distinct experience in the order of salvation.

DISPENSATIONAL PREMILLENNIALISM

The Higher Life current made its greatest contribution to the movement's intellectual architecture through its mediation of the prophetic doctrines of British Plymouth Brethren scholar, John Nelson Darby. The attempt to glean esoteric insights by harmonizing prophetic passages of the Bible had long been a staple of Christian hermeneutics, but Darby's general schema, known as dispensational premillennialism, struck many evangelicals as uniquely definitive. Disseminated and elaborated through prophecy conferences at Niagara and elsewhere, journals such as *Christian Herald and Signs of Our Times,* and by American scholars like Cyrus Ingerson Scofield, dispensationalism quickly hardened into Holiness orthodoxy.

The new theory offered numerous fine points for scholarly dispute, but the most widely accepted version taught that history fell into seven "dispensations"—historical economies or orders—each governed by its own distinctive covenant between God and humanity. Holiness saints found themselves in the sixth dispensation, the Dispensation of Grace or the Church Age. That age had begun with the resurrection of Christ and would conclude with his sudden, secret return to "rapture" his saints, followed immediately by a seven-year period of intense violence and suffering, the Tribulation. The seventh and final dispensation of history would commence with Christ's final Appearing, when, with his army of resurrected saints, he would conquer the forces of Satan and reign during a thousand-year era of peace known as the Millennium. The curtain would then fall on the old secular stage, all would stand before the Final Judgment, the earth would be purged with fire, old things would pass away, a new heaven and a new earth would appear, and the saints would enjoy fellowship with God into the far reaches of eternity.

Dispensationalism had profound implications for the culture of Holiness. For one thing, it lent adherents a certain intellectual gravitas. This was a field of enormous complexity imbued with a scientific aura, wherein close inductive analysis of obscure apocalyptic texts yielded harmonizations that were further elaborated into dense eschatological frameworks complete with charts, diagrams, and other scholarly apparatuses. Particularly as the movement spread beyond the middle class into plainfolk culture—where scholarly disciplines like systematic theology were objects of scorn, not inquiry—dispensationalism offered a valuable outlet for the intellectually inclined.

More importantly, dispensationalism facilitated a mood of intense expectancy, a progressive openness to new insights, and a yearning for the supernatural. First, Holiness saints lay Latter Rain and Evening Light templates over the Church Age. Drawing on proof texts like Deuteronomy 11:14 and popular notions of Near Eastern climatology, they argued by analogy that the "early rain" that had fallen on the Day of Pentecost would be followed at the end of the age by a "latter rain" outpouring of apostolic signs and wonders. Alternately, they suggested that in Palestine the evening light often shone more radiantly than the morning light, so that the spiritual outpouring in their own day might actually excel that which enlivened the Early Church. Hadn't Jesus himself prophesied, "Ye shall do greater things than these"? Both templates projected a restoration of apostolic gifts and power at the end of the Church Age.

Second, dispensationalism built openness to newer and better insights into the very structure of Holiness theology. A trademark of dispensationalism was its notion of progressive revelation, according to which one dispensation built on another to yield an accumulating fullness of divine truth. This constituted an intriguing point of commonality with Protestant liberals of the day, but Holiness saints took it in a quite different direction. For them it meant acquiring new means, methods, and insights sufficient to sweep the world in "a great tidal wave of Holiness." Finally, dispensationalism inspired and sustained intense expectation for the return of Christ. Holiness saints, like generations of millenarians before them, lived "in the shadow of the Second Coming," to use Timothy Weber's poignant phrase. Time was short. Each moment trembled with destiny. A profound sense of urgency thus gripped the movement, prompting extraordinary acts of achievement and sacrifice.

FAITH HEALING

In addition to sanctification and the Second Coming, post–Civil War Holiness placed increasing stress on New Testament signs and wonders. The most important of these was faith healing. Faith healing and other supernatural features of Holiness resonated with the mood of late-Victorian romanticism, which had a fascination for intense experience and the extraordinary. Faith healing also echoed the era's heightened expectations for health and well-being and its growing attention to the physical body. Within this milieu, Holiness came to treat faith healing as less a miraculous demonstration of divine mercy than a fundamental element of full salvation. Drawing on a passage from the First Epistle of Peter, "by his stripes ye are healed," leaders like Simpson argued that Christ through his suffering and sacrificial death had atoned for the sickness of our bodies as well as the sin of our souls.

Faith healing emerged as the centerpiece of the movement's drive to recapitulate the power and praxis of the Apostolic Church, and as such it became a routine feature of Holiness meetings. Furthermore, it generated institutional networks that included an expanding chain of faith homes—centers where the sick could come for extended prayer and spiritual counseling—and the publications and ministries of healing evangelists like Maria Woodworth-Etter, Carrie Judd Montgomery, and John Alexander Dowie.

As important as faith healing may have been to the movement, however, it did not exhaust Holiness views on the bodily form of sanctification. Physical regimens and "health hints" to the holy supplemented the prayer of faith. Countless saints shunned pork, tobacco, coffee, tea, cocoa, chewing gum, and other bad habits not only because they were "worldly," but also because they were injurious to the body, which, as their Bibles told them, was "the temple of the Holy Ghost."

By the late 1880s, the doctrinal cornerstones of the Holiness movement had been codified in the motto of Simpson's Christian Alliance: "Christ our Savior, Sanctifier, Healer, and Coming King." Yet as the saints themselves would have been first to say, doctrine formed the bare outer shell of a sanctified life. Its heart and soul lay in a passionate, transforming encounter with the divine. A richer view of the texture of American Holiness, then, requires a consideration of less tangible qualities such as mood, style, and emphasis, because the social and cultural bequest of Holiness would prove to be as important as its doctrine in shaping the nature and course of American Pentecostalism.

THE SOCIAL AND CULTURAL PARAMETERS OF HOLINESS

As noted, Holiness comprised a diverse, ecumenical movement resistant to precise definition. In many ways, the genius and essence of the movement lay in its syncretism. Holiness drew adherents from a multitude of social, cultural, and ethnic backgrounds and from scores of denominational camps. That diversity was enhanced by the movement's ready exploitation of the nation's rapidly expanding infrastructure, which allowed it to become a truly national phenomenon that self-consciously spanned regional divides, much like other transregional communities of interest—populism, labor unions, reform movements—that built national constituencies along the same corridors. Indeed, Holiness played a notable role in national reunification by drawing Americans from the East, Midwest, and West into an enduring coalition with kindred but sometimes recalcitrant Southerners. Over the decades, the Yankee stigma attached to Southern Holiness faded and a new sacred geography emerged that transcended South and North.

What held true of region applied to the urban-rural divide as well. Holiness carried fresh expressions of old-time religion to the city and urban styles and perspectives to the countryside, prospering in small towns and big cities alike. Finally, Holiness was a genuinely international movement, whose adherents mingled at international conferences in places like Keswick, England, and Gnadau, Germany, and globally on the mission fields of the world. Small wonder then that the Holiness movement considered itself to be a tolerant, inclusive force capable of uniting broad coalitions of Episcopal, Methodist, Presbyterian, Congregational, Baptist, Reformed, and other believers in the pursuit of higher common ground. Holiness would come to be seen as an ecclesiastical belligerent, but it aspired to nothing less than the reunification of the broken body of Christ.

We have already touched on another important aspect of Holiness culture: its progressive cast. Dispensationalism oriented the movement toward the future and opened the door to new and brighter light, but the movement shared other progressive elements as well. These included an instinct for activism, a concern for authentic religious experience, a deep strain of American exceptionalism, and intoxication with the zeitgeist—the spirit of their new and wondrous age with its promise of new and wondrous achievements. And like other progressives, the saints viewed themselves as the antithesis of conservatism, by which they meant the dry, formal, censorious religion of the remembered past.

It may seem strange to describe these progressives as primitivists, but that they were and without contradiction. Indeed, the typically American mode of social adjustment has been to walk backward into the future, eagerly appropriating the material artifacts of modernity while striking a cultural counterpoise that affirms traditional values as it grows more distant from them. Holiness was no exception.

Historians and sociologists identify two kinds of primitivism. The first, chronological primitivism, imagines an original primordium from which the present has fallen and seeks its restoration. The second, cultural primitivism, imagines a primal nature or authenticity that has been attenuated or corrupted and seeks its rejuvenation. Holiness reflected both of these perspectives. It was chronologically primitivist in its zeal to restore the faith and practice of the Apostolic Church. It was culturally primitivist in its pursuit of a superlative Christian life through Holy Ghost baptism.

Primitivism, then, certainly did not mean traditionalism. It meant the time-honored strategy of innovation whereby one's immediate tradition is rejected and replaced on the authority of a putatively primitive one. Dispensationalism, sanctification, and faith healing certainly seemed like innovations to the movement's critics, but to sanctified eyes they were lost treasures that had been refound. Even when a truth did seem new, it was not new *truth,* only truth newly revealed. The devout thus stood with one foot firmly planted on each pole of cosmic history, the present and the primordium, convinced that prophetic symmetry bound the two together in Holiness.

From the 1880s forward, and accelerating in the last decade of the century, Holiness experienced internal tensions that created the true precursor of Pentecostalism. As the movement grew in size and complexity—now with hundreds of Holiness evangelists, scores of associations and periodicals, and perhaps hundreds of thousands of sympathizers—two simultaneous trends emerged. First, growing numbers of plainfolk saints, those with rural and working-class sensibilities, gravitated toward yet more intense expressions of Holiness. Much of the early leadership had come from men and women of privilege, and a strong middle-class air still enveloped elite circles of Holiness. Consequently, plainfolk saints found themselves increasingly alienated both from the mainstream denominations and from more cultured expressions of Holiness.

This radicalization within popular Holiness interacted reciprocally with a second trend: a decisive shift toward independence. As an ecumenical movement, Holiness drew its enthusiasts from the nation's many denominations, most of which did not endorse the new doctrines and practices. Now, more and more denominational saints grew dissatisfied with half-measures and fled these mixed multitudes for independent bodies that fully shared their values and assumptions. Quoting the Second Epistle to the Corinthians ("come out from among

them and be ye separate"), they were known as "comeouters." Their
departures were often greeted as a welcome sight. Holiness saints had
come by then to be associated in the minds of their critics with self-
righteousness and dissension, and the pull of independence was often
matched by the push of exasperated church officials, particularly in
the Methodist Episcopal Church, South, which formally rejected Holiness doctrine in 1894 and moved soon after to restrict the circulation of
Holiness evangelists.

The ranks of independent Holiness swelled as older departures like
the Wesleyan Methodist Church and the Free Methodist Church, and
recent upstarts such as the Salvation Army, the Christian Alliance, and
Daniel Warner's Church of God (Indiana)—also known as the Evening Light Saints—were joined by a steady stream of new ventures.
The Church of the Nazarene (Los Angeles), the Independent Holiness
Church of Texas, the Metropolitan Church Association (Chicago), the
International Holiness Union and Prayer League (Cincinnati), the
Church of God in Christ (Tennessee), the Fire-Baptized Holiness Asso-
ciation (Iowa), and the Holiness Church of North Carolina are only
a few of the small sects that joined scores of missions, faith homes,
and evangelistic ministries in the growing world of independent
Holiness.

The leading comeouters were almost by definition persons of
independent thought and action, assertive and entrepreneurial, less
susceptible than their peers to social pressure, less willing to compromise, more willing to carry convictions to their logical ends as they
calculated them. They overwhelmingly shared the egalitarian, plainfolk values of working-class America, and for many this, as noted,
lay at the root of their dual alienation from mainline denominations
and mainstream Holiness. Particularly in their dispute with mainstream Holiness, gentility, not doctrine, provided the offense. Zealots
believed that mainstream figures like Moody had grown lukewarm.
Their religion was decent, sober, orderly, and orthodox. Indeed, the
worst thing about it was its respectability. A fervent religious experience "once hot with holy love" now lay buried beneath "a smooth
shroud of virtue." One uncharitable critic labeled it "the polar snow
fields of tame holiness."[1]

At issue were powerful cultural traditions that defined proper religious and social behavior. For plainfolk Americans the decorum and
grace of cultured religion did not evoke images of truth, beauty, and
order, but rather of social pretension and spiritual impotence. As
churchly America gentrified, then, it drew further from the cultural
idioms that spoke to its populist constituency. Independent Holiness

would be that constituency's champion. These saints liked to refer to themselves as "radical," and it was an apt description. Together they created the world of radical Holiness, the hothouse of American Pentecostalism.

RADICAL HOLINESS

While class defined in Marxist terms has never been the basis for social cohesion in the United States, the opposite is true of class as an expression of cultural difference. Class in that sense has typically been a precondition for such cohesion, so that much of the nation's religious differentiation still falls along class lines. It is not surprising then that radical Holiness rhetoric reflected the deep-seated cultural antagonisms inherent in populist egalitarianism. Radical Holiness vividly recapitulated one of the most universal and enduring features of plainfolk culture—a bristling repudiation of the patterns of deference and polite civilities that sustained privilege and social hierarchy. Like early Christians and 16th-century Quakers, radical saints refused to show "respect of persons." They sneered at "aristocratic" churches and conspicuously aligned with "the despised, the poor, the downcast, the outcast." Theirs was the language of divine reversal according to which God had upended rich and poor, great and small.[2] Thomas Nelson, founder of the Pentecostal Bands of the World and editor of the *Pentecostal Herald* (Indianapolis), declaimed that "vital Christianity" could only exist among the "virtuous poor." Wealth, like wickedness, extinguished "the vital spark of real Christianity." What could his readers expect to find among the wealthy members of a "large, popular, fashionable, city church?" Only "a rich man's tomb" where "a dead Christ is embalmed in the spices of worldly respectability."[3]

Nothing focused these deeply seated class antagonisms more effectively than did a second important feature of radical Holiness: religious ecstasy. The saints called it "shouting" and proudly defended it. The ecstatic frenzy of holy possession composed a rich kinetic symbolism that demarcated social and religious boundaries with keen efficiency, but it repaid its practitioners with much more than boundary maintenance. Visible evidence of God's validating presence for the community, palpable assurance for the disquieted soul, a dense catechism on the nature of the divine-human relationship for all—this was the kind of bedrock spiritual evidence that turned "I think so" into "I *know* so" religion. One saint boiled it down even further. "Falling, screaming, shouting, running, jumping, laughing" are "manifestations of the Holy Ghost," wrote Abner Backmon Crumpler, founder of the

Holiness Church of North Carolina. "A corpse never moves."[4] Ecstasy offered proof of life.

The same threads that bound religious ecstasy to issues of class and religion tied them both to the question of race. "There are some people who think that nobody but poor folks and 'niggers' ever shout," fumed Crumpler. If so, he added, "it is because nobody but the poor folks and the 'niggers' have anything to shout about."[5] The most radical reaches of Holiness were also the most integrated, and for good reason. Its theology of the poor necessarily enhanced the spiritual status of those who were by far the nations' most viciously oppressed, and religious ecstasy formed an index of divine presence that functioned independently of social or material criteria. An illiterate African American "full of the Holy Ghost," wrote William Baxter Godbey, one of the movement's most prolific authors, "has more Gospel in his soul...than a whole car-load of plug-hatted theologians."[6]

Racism was far too pervasive not to exist among white advocates of Holiness, but it typically appeared as the polite, garden-variety racism intrinsic to late Victorian "common sense." Most white evangelists aimed for the middle ground between Galatians 3:28 ("There is neither Jew nor Greek...bond nor free...male nor female") and Jim Crow, ministering to and with African Americans but without directly challenging the day-to-day norm of racial segregation. That being said, radical Holiness did open the door to truly revolutionary thinking, as when Dowie averred that, since the disintegration of primal humanity into races was a consequence of the fall, only miscegenation, the racial reintegration of humanity, could restore humanity's original form. Viewed as a whole, radical Holiness fell short of 21st-century racial ideals, but it stood out in its own day for its racial tolerance and for the degree to which it allowed African Americans to share and shape a predominately Anglo-American movement.

Life in the religious margins offered even greater social freedom to Holiness women. From itinerant celebrities like Woodworth-Etter to local preachers like Annie May Fisher and Mary Lee Cagle, women took prominent positions alongside men in every region of the country at a time when only four states offered women full voting rights. But even more surprising than the fact of women's ministry was its nature. At precisely the time when anxiety over the perceived softening of American manhood was provoking new assertions of masculinity, the gospel that Holiness women preached, and the way they preached it, challenged Victorian domesticity at its core.

By the end of the 19th century, increased stress on health, fitness, and the primal virtues of wilderness had merged with American jingoism to promote a more rugged ideal of manliness, as popularly embodied in the person of Teddy Roosevelt, the "Rough Rider." Radical Holiness, as a general rule, had more in common with the new, exaggerated manliness than with the old sentimentalism. Holiness demanded unflinching personal bravery, unyielding spiritual strength, and the cheerful endurance of physical hardship. "Men Wanted," blared one solicitation for Holiness workers, "with muscles of iron and nerves of steel, in whose tremendous grasp baptized iniquity whimpers like a whipped child."[7] If the response was typical of Holiness, many of the "men" who responded were women, and they attacked iniquity with all the vehemence of their male comrades. Women like Alma White were full shooting members of God's Rough Riders and they blasted the fortress of hell with heavy ammunition. Radical Holiness allowed women to assume prophetic stances and to employ militant language that were, in the idiom of the time, nothing short of "manly." Gender roles were not, and would never be, erased. Women still faced barriers to full ordination in many associations. But radical Holiness drew women into active ministry and empowered them to adopt public styles and modes of expression that were thought in the wider society to be the exclusive province of men.

Many of the most vivid and controversial traits of radical Holiness reflected a simple intensification of the perfectionist impulse intrinsic to Holiness as such. Entire sanctification, for example, expressed a yearning to shatter the limits of human frailty and enter a realm far beyond that known to run-of-the-mill Christians. Holiness would not settle for ordinary religion, or an ordinary life. Radical saints, however, stood out for the visceral degree to which they scorned mediocrity and for their refusal to abide it in themselves or in others. "I would thou wert cold or hot," the resurrected Christ told the Laodiceans in the Book of Revelation. "Because thou art lukewarm ... I will spue thee out of my mouth." Radical saints took these words to heart. "My whole being has revolted against defeat," exclaimed Seth Cook Rees. "Win or die!"[8] So win they did. In 1896, Crumpler boasted 9 years of sinless perfection. In 1891, the Quaker Amos Kenworthy had counted 21.

Sinless perfection would have been a tall order for anyone, but for themselves the saints raised the bar. These were ethical rigorists of the first water who routed the seven deadly sins and then pursued imperfection to its most distant outposts. "I verily believe artificial flowers, face powders and feathers are a mark of the beast" declared one female saint.[9] Pork, tea, coffee, and cocoa came under fire, and many, perhaps most, of these faith healing advocates counted medicine among things verboten. Even neckties drew stray rounds of holy fire.

As ethical rigorism suggests, radical Holiness had a militant side. In the material realm, many saints were strict pacifists who would obey Christ and turn the other cheek if physically assaulted. But in the spiritual and rhetorical realms, they were heavily armed combatants. "I am in for war—war to the hilt," proclaimed Benjamin Hardin Irwin. "And I just love it."[10] As Kenworthy explained, "We are an army, not a polite lady-club."[11] Militancy, of course, provoked like-minded reactions in others, but the saints seemed to relish those validating experiences of persecution. "What an honor to be jeered at, hated, despised, reviled," Frank Sandford exclaimed. "Thereby you may prove yourself 'worthy' of robes such as the Son of God Himself wears."[12]

But this told only half of a paradoxical story. Militancy and ethical severity shared space with heartfelt pronouncements of tolerance and eloquent expressions of humility and mystical union. So long as the Holiness essentials of salvation and sanctification were proclaimed with sufficient force, the saints could abide a surprising range of doctrinal latitude. Moreover, some of the movement's most prominent figures defended that latitude by elaborating a pietistic epistemology, reminiscent of Friedrich Schleiermacher, that located religious truth in a transcendent, precognitive realm of immediate experience. When minister and educator Stephen Olin Garrison assembled *Forty Witnesses* to Holiness from six denominations, he cautioned against expecting uniformity of expression. The distinction between self and the definition of self, truth and the definition of truth meant that even "the most devout minds" might not agree on "the terminology...of deeper religious experiences." Holiness, he insisted, was "at war with exclusiveness of doctrinal statement." George Watson phrased it more eloquently: True religion was "a heart quality, a soul essence, too fluid to be held in by words." Indeed, "A hundred earnest souls may plead 'refining fire go through my heart,' yet no two of them have the same conception of what it really means."[13] At the far depth of the devout heart, dogmatic propositions had no place.

Pietistic epistemology opened the door to profound mysticism as well as to ecumenical latitude. Watson, one of the movement's most beloved and widely read authors, returned often to this theme. Sanctification was but the first step on an intimate journey toward "sweetest union with divine nature." Saints were urged to pass through the portal of humility, that "sweetly sorrowful, sadly beautiful flame of self-abnegation," into "a deep, interior vision of the soul of Jesus."[14] Here was the holy warrior as mystic saint, plunged into a contemplative sea where divine wrath and divine love merged into a single ineffable nature.

Passionate perfectionism also shaped the institutional manifestations of radical Holiness. Many saints rejected anything that smacked of human authority in churchly matters, enthroning the Holy Ghost as their only teacher and the Holy Bible as their only rule of faith. Along with formalism, "man-made" creeds, and empty rituals, the saints denounced ecclesiastical hierarchy and many resisted even minimal efforts to organize radical forces, fearing what they called "ecclesiasticism," the deadening attempt to capture the Holy Ghost in a human invention.

Furthermore, radical saints generally understood the person and work of the Holy Ghost in terms of extemporaneous inspiration, irrupting unpredictably in male or female, young or old, clergy or laity. The Spirit was a divine wind that "bloweth where it listeth," they learned from the Gospel of John, and "thou...canst not tell whence it cometh, and whither it goeth." Indeed, at its margins radical Holiness occasioned visions of pneumatological theocracy unlike anything seen since the English Midlands in the 17th century. As with the early Quakers, they too wished to banish every sign of the human hand in utter surrender to the divine will and way. Even when human authority was banished in theory, of course, it continued to exist in practice, though dangerously unrecognized as such. Nonetheless, something vital was developing in radical Holiness, and it would have a profound impact on the Pentecostal movement to come.

A final trait to notice in this regard relates to the stark supernaturalism, and the sheer intensity, cultivated within radical Holiness. Sanctification, faith healing, and religious ecstasy were part and parcel of a world replete with supernatural marvels. Indeed, supernatural is perhaps a misleading term, since it suggests a bifurcated cosmos in which the extraordinary interrupts the mundane. Perhaps it is more accurate to say that radical Holiness sacralized its entire cosmos, collapsing natural and supernatural into a single unitary order. The saints thus lived in an open, not closed, universe, within which every daily moment, every ordinary thing gleamed with miraculous potential.

For example, radical missionaries and evangelists often adopted the "life on faith lines" popularized by philanthropist George Mueller, according to which one should confide in and rely on God and God alone to supply life's basic needs. Daily life thus became a sacred drama and every meal an instance of divine provision. No need was too small, no obstacle too great, to submit to divine intervention. And power became an obsession. Mere insight and wise counsel were not adequate to ministry in this kind of movement. One needed "manliness and Godliness fused into electric effectiveness by the fire of the

Holy Ghost," as one writer described Rees.[15] Radical Holiness had fashioned a world of power and wonder in which the miraculous was routine, the routine miraculous.

For all of this there remained a deeply pragmatic countercurrent in radical Holiness, particularly when it came to evangelistic strategy and the use of material resources. Radical saints possessed a knack for marketing and self-promotion along with an intuitive sense of how to apply modern technology to social mobilization. Modern modes of transportation and communication, for example, were not parts of the world from which they separated. Rather, they were providential means brought forth in the fullness of time to make possible a great worldwide revival that would foretoken the Second Coming of Jesus Christ.

Peripatetic saints crisscrossed the nation and the globe, while scores of printing presses churned out literature for mass distribution. Holiness journals served as movement clearinghouses, sharing news, publicizing events, and printing weekly train schedules. Bible schools and training institutes offered practical, short-term courses designed to convey essential skills and deliver workers to the ministry or mission field as expeditiously as possible. Aggressively entrepreneurial, mobile, and inventive, radical Holiness nimbly responded to demographic shifts, particularly within its plainfolk market. The Holy Ghost blew where it willed, but it willed to blow in directions that neatly matched the contours of a changing nation.

Radical Holiness, then, formed a movement of dense range and complexity. Here were belligerents who heaped vituperation on apostates even as they called them to humbly follow Perfect Love, schismatics who mourned division in the body of Christ, ethical rigorists who denounced legalism as among the gravest of sins. They searched the secret places of their hearts with mystical introspection, yet practiced the most extroverted religious demonstrations. They preached from soapboxes on sidewalks and street corners yet used every modern means to spread their message around the block and around the world. It was a potent religious compound that contained the detriments as well as the benefits of diversity. Unity would prove elusive, change would be guaranteed, but it held almost limitless potential for growth.

PATHWAYS TO PENTECOSTALISM

As the new century approached, a growing certainty prevailed among radical saints that the full panoply of Apostolic signs and wonders had been restored in their midst. The use of Pentecostal terminology grew more common, reflecting an increased fixation on the Book of Acts and an increased expectation that the marvels recorded therein were now being replicated. Across the country kindred spirits formed circles and networks, cultural corridors that would soon become the pathways to Pentecostalism.

In the Northeast, key points along this emerging nexus included Frank Sandford's compound at Shiloh, Maine (with his journal, *Tongues of Fire*); the Christian Workers Union in Massachusetts; Simpson's Christian and Missionary Alliance (and its network of local affiliates, its regional camp meetings, and its training center at Nyack, New York); the Elim ministry in Rochester; and the Association of Pentecostal Churches of America.

In the Midwest, Dowie had transformed his Chicago ministry into an exhilarating Holiness utopia at nearby Zion, Illinois; Nelson's Pentecostal Bands of the World barnstormed Indiana and shared the Good News through his *Pentecostal Herald*; the Cincinnati-based International Holiness Union and Prayer League, directed by Martin Wells Knapp and Seth Rees, welcomed thousands of earnest seekers, including a young itinerate evangelist, William Seymour, who had recently affiliated with Warner's Evening Light Saints.

Further west, Charles Parham founded Beth-el Healing Home and Bible School in Topeka, Kansas, and published the *Apostolic Faith*; Irwin's Fire Baptized Holiness Association, begun in Iowa, spread rapidly throughout the Midwest and South; Denver was enlivened by Alma White's Pentecostal Union; and the Bay Area ministry of Carrie Judd Montgomery, together with the Southern California Holiness Association and Phineas Bresee's Church of the Nazarene, bracketed the Golden State.

In the South, Crumpler's Holiness Church of North Carolina shared the state with Ambrose Jessup Tomlinson and a fledgling circle of Holiness saints that would soon become the Church of God; the Church of God in Christ, formed in Tennessee by Charles Harrison Mason and Charles Price Jones, complemented the Kentucky work of Henry Clay Morrison and his *Pentecostal Herald*; and from South Carolina, John M. Pike's *Way of Faith*, the region's most influential journal, heartily cheered the radical line. By no means would all of these institutions or figures endorse Pentecostalism, but they along with scores of others provided the scaffolding on which the new movement would build.

By the turn of the century, a significant minority within these circles had come to espouse yet a third blessing: the Baptism of Fire. Its greatest champion was Irwin, whose Fire-Baptized Holiness Association had by 1898 spread to nine states and two Canadian provinces. Advocates of fire baptism cited John the Baptist's prophecy that the Coming One would baptize "with the Holy Ghost and with fire," which for them implied two separate baptisms, one with the Holy Ghost and another with fire. The ground had been prepared, then, for further works of grace and a threefold *ordo salutis.*

Finally, scattered reports of glossolalia—under Sandford at Shiloh, in the mountains of North Carolina—began to appear. Were these the other tongues spoken of on the Day of Pentecost? New truths and deeper revelations, sealed up for the Last Days, were unfolding before their eyes. A full restoration of Pentecostal gifts was underway. It was a wondrous time to be a saint, alive.

NOTES

1. George D. Watson, "Lukewarmness," *Way of Faith,* June 10, 1896, 1; Benjamin Hardin Irwin, "The Abiding Fire," *Way of Faith,* December 16, 1896, 1.

2. Vinson Synan, *Old Time Power* (Franklin Springs, GA: Advocate Press, 1973), 69.

3. Thomas H. Nelson, *Pentecostal Herald* (Indianapolis), December 15, 1901, 5.

4. Abner Backmon Crumpler, "Manifestations of the Holy Ghost," *Holiness Advocate,* September 15, 1903, 3.

5. Abner Backmon Crumpler, "Sermon on Shouting," *Holiness Advocate,* August 1, 1903.

6. Quoted in Randall Stephens, *The Fire Spreads: Holiness and Pentecostalism in the American South* (Cambridge, MA: Harvard University Press, 2008), 98.

7. Thomas H. Nelson, *Pentecostal Herald,* June 1, 1894, 2.

8. Paul S. Rees, *Seth Cook Rees: The Warrior Saint* (Indianapolis, IN: Pilgrim Book Room, 1934).

9. Berta Maxwell, *Holiness Advocate,* October 15, 1903, 8.

10. Benjamin Hardin Irwin, "Purcell, Indian Territory," *Way of Faith,* July 8, 1896, 1.

11. Lydia M. Williams-Cammack and Truman C. Kenworthy, *Life and Works of Amos M. Kenworthy* (Richmond, IN: Nicholson Printing, 1918), 233.

12. Frank Sandford, *Everlasting Gospel,* January 1, 1901, 8.

13. Stephen Olin Garrison, ed., *Forty Witnesses* (Philadelphia [?], 1888), 5–6; George Watson, *Soul Food: Being Chapters on the Interior Life* (Cincinnati, OH: Revivalist Office, 1896), 132; George Watson, *Way of Faith*, November 6, 1895, 2.

14. Watson, *Soul Food*, 128–136.

15. Rees, *Seth Cook Rees*, 45.

CHAPTER 2

A New Religion for a New Millennium

The gathering mood of prophetic expectancy within radical Holiness peaked at the threshold of the new millennium. Two of the movement's most notorious celebrities proclaimed themselves to be Elijah the Prophet, the signal figure whose appearance, according to dispensationalist theory, would herald Christ's Second Coming just as John the Baptist had heralded his first. John Dowie, the Chicago-based healing evangelist and founder of Zion City, Illinois, made his self-disclosure in June 1901. Six months later, Frank Sandford, apostolic wonder worker and head of Shiloh, the Holiness commune and training center near Durham, Maine, registered a counterclaim. The true measure of the mood within radical Holiness, however, is not so much that the claims were made as that thousands of devout saints found them plausible. Meanwhile, within that fertile bed of expectancy the Pentecostal movement was born, though few at the time took notice.

To seek the origins of Pentecostalism is not the same as to seek the origins of glossolalia. As noted, late 19th-century Holiness had nurtured a growing fixation on Pentecostal texts like the Acts of the Apostles and Mark 16, which correlated with a growing use of Pentecostal terminology. Glossolalia, then, loomed as something very near a textual imperative for the movement, and indeed outbursts had appeared in the United States as early as the 1890s. The question, though, is not who first spoke in tongues but who first made something of it. Where, how, and through whose agency did glossolalia, which might have been incorporated into Holiness as a welcome addition to its panoply of signs and wonders, become instead the symbolic catalyst of a new movement? Viewed in these terms, the origins of Pentecostalism trace to a small Midwestern fellowship under the direction of Charles Fox Parham. Having said this, a note of caution is in order. Pentecostalism, like Holiness, would have no definitive center or individual. It was not that kind of movement.

CHARLES PARHAM AND THE BIRTH OF PENTECOSTALISM

The Iowa-born, Kansas-reared Parham began his ministry in 1893 as a 20-year-old lay pastor in the Methodist Episcopal Church. Already devoted to Holiness teaching and convinced that he himself had been miraculously healed of rheumatic fever, Parham soon left Methodism for a career as an independent Holiness evangelist. In 1896 he married Sarah Thistlethwaite, a Holiness Quaker, and two years later the young couple founded Beth-el Healing Home in Topeka, Kansas, where they also published a newspaper, *The Apostolic Faith.*

By the late 1890s Parham had apparently embraced B. H. Irwin's concept of fire baptism, and years later he would fondly recall the Irwin days when "people screamed until you could hear them for three miles on a clear night, and until the blood vessels stood out like whip cords."[1] But as a man of restless temperament and mixed religious heritage, he continued to explore spiritual insights and alliances as he found them. In the summer of 1900 Parham briefly allied with Sandford following a revival held by the latter in Topeka. The two shared pulpits on the evangelistic trail, and Parham spent several weeks at Sandford's compound at Shiloh where glossolalia had been reported as early as 1897 and had continued sporadically thereafter. When it came to apostolic power, no one outdid Sandford. Life at Shiloh, as viewed through the pages of *Tongues of Fire*, composed a stark tableau of potent signs and wonders. It was the kind of place where the dead were raised, the disobedient struck dead, and warrior-saints battled "demons by the millions."

Parham's time at Shiloh surely whetted his interest in glossolalia, but it was only one stop in a three-month stint of Holy Ghost tourism that also included a visit to Dowie's Christian Catholic Church in Chicago. The renowned Scottish-born Australian faith healer had immigrated to the United States in 1888, and by 1900, though not yet Elijah the Prophet, had begun to lay the groundwork for Zion City, a socioreligious utopia north of Chicago that would eventually attract upwards of 6,000 inhabitants. Parham would eventually draw up his own designs for Zion, but in 1900 he was just passing through. By the time Parham returned to Topeka that September, he had surveyed ventures associated with an array of Holiness notables ranging from A. J. Gordon and A. B. Simpson to Holiness Quaker John Walter Malone, in addition to Dowie and Sandford.[2]

Back in Topeka, Parham promptly leased an abandoned mansion and set up his own communal training center, Bethel Bible School, where he and approximately 40 residents pursued a yet deeper experience that he was now sure awaited the earnest seeker. Reportedly, Parham instructed his students to search the book of Acts for the verifying signs of baptism with the Holy Ghost. As Pentecostals today are quick to point out, the gift of tongues either explicitly or implicitly accompanies every instance of Spirit baptism recorded therein, beginning with the archetypal account of the Day of Pentecost in Acts 2:4, when the disciples "were all filled with the Holy Ghost, and began to speak in other tongues, as the Spirit gave them utterance." Perhaps it is not surprising, then, that under Parham's tutelage the group reached a simple but severe conclusion: glossolalia constituted the "initial physical evidence," the sine qua non of baptism with the Holy Ghost.

Whether the group reached that conclusion before or after glossolalia erupted at Bethel is disputed, but erupt it did on New Year's Day 1901, when one Agnes Ozman spoke in tongues. Within days Parham and about half of the student body had followed suit. A minor frenzy of evangelization ensued, with mixed results, as Parham and his students spread the news of what they deemed to be the first full outpouring of the Holy Spirit since that aforementioned Day of Pentecost.

Parham's systematizing mind quickly knit these events into a coherent theological framework within which glossolalia played three essential roles. First, glossolalia in fact meant xenolalia, the miraculous ability to speak an unstudied foreign language. As such it represented a utilitarian gift bestowed to facilitate the rapid evangelization of the world prior to Christ's return. Second, glossolalia was the sign that inevitably accompanied and verified Spirit baptism. Finally, it constituted the seal of the Bride of Christ, the identifying mark that set apart the true church for her soon-coming bridegroom.

Those who followed would amend this formula. The notion of tongues as an eschatological seal for the church would be largely abandoned, and though Pentecostals would continue to distinguish between the sign and the gift of tongues, the emphasis on xenolalia quickly receded. But Parham's second proposition, the bold assertion that glossolalia alone constituted the initial evidence of Holy Ghost Baptism, would survive as a pillar of mainstream Pentecostal orthodoxy.

The full import of these new insights must have taken a while to sink in. Baptism with the Holy Spirit was not entire sanctification but rather a third blessing subsequent to it. And glossolalia accompanied every valid baptism. These were provocative innovations, a doctrinal double twist that in two fell swoops disqualified the Spirit baptisms of everyone else in the Holiness movement. Not all tongues-speakers would accept Parham's exclusivist views, but glossolalia would hence-forth serve as a visible (and audible) line of demarcation. A distinctive practice plus a distinctive doctrine equaled the makings of a distinctive movement.

THE APOSTOLIC FAITH

Over the next several years Parham and associates proclaimed what they called the Apostolic Faith through much of Kansas, Missouri, Texas, and Arkansas, but the new doctrine was a hard sell and the movement ebbed more than it flowed. In late 1903 and early 1904, however, Parham's fortunes turned. Spectacular healing campaigns in Galena, Kansas; Joplin, Missouri; and Old Orchard, Texas, brought hundreds of converts and renewed momentum. Soon, an expanding network of Apostolic Faith Missions began to take shape. The area around Houston, Texas, proved especially receptive, and in the summer of 1905 Parham and a band of workers made it their base of operations. Like other Holiness saints, Parham despised ecclesiasticism, which in the Holiness lexicon meant anything resembling the denominational strictures and structures that comeouters had just departed from. But in the interests of fellowship and apostolic order, he nonetheless took rudimentary steps to organize his growing Apostolic Faith Movement by appointing regional directors and designating himself as its Projector.

Parham's movement had turned the corner but it made only a minor splash in the Holiness press. By contrast, two contemporaneous revivals, one in Wales in 1904–1905 and another in India in 1905–1906, riveted sanctified readers around the world. The Welsh revival, celebrated in scores of breathless tracts and newspaper accounts, electrified saints with reports of mass conversions and startling manifestations of the Holy Spirit. Although nominally led by Evan Roberts, the meetings were said to proceed with utter spontaneity, unguided by human hand. These accounts helped spark similar outpourings in India, where just as in Wales penitent sinners vented "great anguish of soul" in "screams and groans," falling unconscious or writhing on the ground, only to rise "singing, clapping" and "dancing" in victory. And through it all ran the perfect harmony of a Divine Composer. "Hundreds pray audibly at the same time," one observer noted, "and yet there is no sense of disorder or confusion."[3]

These wonderments persuaded many saints that the final worldwide revival was underway. In Los Angeles, a fiercely ascetic evangelist and reporter, Frank Bartleman, read the news and dashed off wide-eyed editorials for John Pike's South Carolina–based *Way of Faith*. "The Spirit is brooding over our land again as at creation's dawn," he enthused. "The fiat of God goes forth. 'Let there be light.'"[4] A fellow Angeleno, the Reverend Joseph Smale of First Baptist Church, traveled to Wales to witness the events firsthand. The experience transformed his ministry, and he returned to found the First New Testament Church, a place where radical saints like Bartleman and Florence Crawford, a locally known rescue mission and temperance activist, could pray for a like outpouring in the City of Angels.

Back in Houston, Parham and his team continued to spread the Apostolic Faith throughout the summer of 1905, laying siege to the city via mass meetings, street preaching, door-to-door evangelism, and ministry among the down and out. They also sought inroads into the African American community, where Parham found a key ally in Lucy Farrow, a Holiness preacher and niece of Frederick Douglass who served as his cook and coworker. When Parham left that fall for an extended campaign in southeastern Kansas, he took Farrow with him. Farrow, in turn, entrusted her small congregation to a Holiness minister in his mid-30s by the name of William Seymour.

Like Parham, Seymour arrived in Houston with a theologically diverse and geographically wide-ranging background. Born in Louisiana in 1870 to ex-slave parents, he later moved to Indianapolis, where he made his way into Holiness and affiliated with Daniel Warner's Evening Light Saints. Between 1895 and 1905, Seymour traveled widely and encountered a number of important Holiness leaders, including Church of God in Christ cofounder C. P. Jones and the evangelist and former Zion elder, John Graham Lake. By the late 1890s, his closest association appears to have been with Knapp and Rees's International Holiness Union and Prayer League, whose God's Bible School he reportedly attended.

Seymour reached Houston in 1903, where his character and ability caught the eye of African American Holiness leaders like Farrow, who now offered him her pulpit. By all accounts Seymour handled the task well. Indeed, he left one visitor, Neely Terry, so thoroughly impressed that when she returned to her home in Los Angeles she recommended him to other members of her storefront mission, which would soon have a pastoral vacancy.

By the time Parham's evangelistic team returned that fall, Farrow had received her own Pentecost. She eagerly shared the good news with Seymour, who now joined her in attending Parham's meetings. When Parham opened a short-term Bible school in nearby Brunner, Texas, at the start of the new year, Seymour enrolled, although in deference to Jim Crow laws, he took a seat just outside the classroom door. The curriculum included a large share of hands-on training, which meant that Parham and Seymour—who now accepted the Pentecostal doctrine though he had not received the experience—shared pulpits and street corners on several occasions during the early weeks of 1906.

Scarcely a month into his course of study, however, a call from Los Angeles interrupted Seymour's training. Neely Terry's home church, a small storefront mission at Ninth and Santa Fe affiliated with the Holiness Church Association of Southern California, was about to lose its pastor and founder, Julia Hutchins, to the mission fields of Liberia. Now, based on prayerful consideration, the group looked to Seymour as her replacement. So it was that, at Hutchins's invitation and over Parham's objections, Seymour headed west for a date with destiny.

On February 22, 1906, Seymour arrived in Los Angeles, where he found a diverse and rapidly growing metropolis of a quarter-million residents whose Holiness community had been both splintered and energized by intense millennial expectation. For a preacher like Seymour, the city held every promise of success, though he found little at Ninth and Santa Fe. Neither Hutchins nor other leaders in the Holiness Church Association would abide his new teaching on tongues, and in early March they expelled him from the mission. Undeterred, Seymour took his message to sympathetic homes, eventually settling in a cottage on North Bonnie Brae Street, where his exuberant meetings drew the attention of the local Holiness community, white and black, and attracted visitors like Bartleman and the Reverend Arthur Osterberg.

Meanwhile, Lucy Farrow had arrived from Houston to assist her former associate, and on April 9, a worshiper under her superintendence experienced Holy Ghost baptism and began to speak in tongues. It was the breakthrough Seymour had been longing for. Within days, dozens of others, including Seymour himself, had secured the experience, and the swelling crowds that flocked to the portentous spectacle forced a search for new accommodations. They found them at 312 Azusa Street, in what is now the Little Tokyo district of Los Angeles, where an abandoned African Methodist Episcopal church was reborn as the Apostolic Faith Mission.

The potent revival that erupted there, with its ecstatic frenzies, outbursts of glossolalia, and racial mingling, gripped the secular as well as the Holiness press. On April 18, only days after the mission opened its doors, the *Los Angeles Daily Times* mocked the "Weird Babel of Tongues" and "howlings of the worshipers" it found there. That same day, a devastating earthquake jolted San Francisco. Saints like Bartleman saw the coincidence as a providential omen and trumpeted the earthquake and their revival as God's "Last Call" to repentance.

Azusa Street rapidly mushroomed into a global phenomenon, drawing the curious, the censorious, and the sincere from across the country and around the world. For the better part of three years, crowds of up to 1,500 pressed into and around the modest mission, with meetings at their peak running from mid-morning to midnight, seven days a week. A who's who of Holiness luminaries made pilgrimages to Azusa Street, and many cast their lot with the new movement. In addition, emissaries from Azusa fanned out to found spin-off missions or convert existing ones. By the time the revival subsided, it had secured its place as the epic and epochal event of early Pentecostalism.[5]

While revival raged at Azusa Street, Parham deliberated. He had planned to visit Azusa in September 1906, since he viewed Seymour as his protégé and both regarded the work in Los Angeles as an extension of Parham's Apostolic Faith Movement. Exactly what it meant to be part of such a movement, however, remained an open question. At the last minute, though, Parham changed course to pursue a tantalizing opportunity in Chicago, where Dowie's work lay in ruins.

At its peak, Zion had been home to thousands of residents, and the Christian Catholic Church had once claimed as many as 200,000 followers worldwide. Now scandal, bankruptcy, and a debilitating illness had forced the prophet's removal and the sale of Zion City. With Zion in disarray, Parham reached for the harvest in Dowie's demise. And harvest he did. Hundreds of Dowie's followers, including much of Zion's leadership, joined forces with Parham; many would later rise to prominence in the Pentecostal movement.

Bolstered by fresh infusions from Zion, Parham now bestrode an Apostolic Faith Movement claiming as many as 10,000 adherents. Finally, in October and with Seymour's blessing, he traveled to Los Angeles to assert his authority over that branch of his movement. Counterfactual historians are left to ponder what the course of Pentecostalism might have been had Parham commended Seymour and

his work, gaining influence through a welcoming yet gently paterna-
listic hand. But that was not to be. Instead, Parham launched a racially
tinged assault on what he deemed fanaticism and religious anarchy
at Azusa Street and demanded reforms that included the outright
dismissal of many of Seymour's key aides. Seymour responded by
recanting an earlier acknowledgment of Parham's authority and
declaring the Holy Ghost to be the mission's only leader.

The Seymour-Parham breakup marked the beginning of the end of
Parham's prominence within the movement. As it turned out, Azusa
Street's days were also numbered. The peak of the revival spanned
from 1906 through 1908, with another surge in 1911. Shortly thereafter, its star faded. From the vantage point of Pentecostal history, however, that hardly mattered, because by then the movement had already
taken wing.

PENTECOSTAL SPIRITUALITY

As Pentecostalism spread and ramified, it naturally took many
forms, but after 1906 the dominant currents of its spirituality bore the
imprint of Azusa Street, which had in turn carried forward the more
unfettered impulses of Holiness. Pentecostals sought utter submission
to the Holy Spirit, whose presence they associated with spontaneity,
emotional intensity, and divine surprise. If the Holy Spirit were
truly in charge, many believed, worship would give no visible sign
of human orchestration. It would, however, involve a great deal of
human participation, including boisterous and simultaneous prayer,
fervent testimony, rituals of healing, outbursts of holy delirium like
"shouting" or "dancing in the Spirit," and the trancelike experience of
being "slain in the Spirit." In addition to these standard Holiness exer-
tions, however, Pentecostals restructured their inheritance in subtle
but substantive ways.

To begin with, the dramatic performance of tongues and the interpretation of tongues (an inspired translation of glossolalia into the common
language) quickly emerged as the de facto centerpiece of Pentecostal
worship. These were fluid entities, however, with meanings that were
never precisely defined. Was the "sign" of tongues that attested one's
Spirit baptism different from the "gift" of tongues that one used in
worship and private prayer? Was glossolalia a literal foreign tongue—
xenolalia—or the heavenly language of angels? Should it be subdivided
into categories of sacred speech: the language of praise; the language
of travail; the soul's deepest articulations; the prophetic voice of God
speaking to the individual or through the individual to the community

of saints? For the most part, Pentecostals seemed content to leave these questions unanswered. The spiritual terrain remained unmapped, which allowed the various possibilities to coexist within a single framework of Pentecostal worship.

Glossolalic rituals, furthermore, occurred within a matrix of complementary behaviors that were also new or at least perceived to be so, such as the charismatic performance of drama, music, and song. Worshipers might enact impromptu pantomimes illustrating a sermon or dramatizing a message given in tongues. They might play musical instruments under the power of the Holy Ghost or break forth in synchronized melodies known as the heavenly chorus. "No regular order, and yet perfect order," wrote one leader of a 1909 service in Tennessee. "The singing was led by the Holy Ghost," he explained. "One would lead a song and someone else...would take up the next verse and the whole congregation would join."[6] To enraptured saints, the free flow of worship gave proof of God's sovereign and validating presence.

Another proof of God's presence, the element of divine surprise, came in several varieties. One involved the marvel of transcending ordinary social parameters—as, for example, when saints as old as 100 or as young as 7 preached sermons. But the condition for the possibility of such marvels rested in an underlying destabilization of liturgical order. Particularly in the movement's earlier and more liminal years, egalitarianism and radical pneumatology converged to shatter the clerical monopoly on authoritative speech, producing an open pulpit ideal modeled best by Seymour himself. At Azusa Street, "no one knew what might be coming," Bartleman reminisced. "The Lord was liable to burst through any one." Divine inspiration was the sole prerequisite for public utterance. "Someone would finally get up, anointed for the message," he explained. "It might be a child, a woman, or a man. It might be from the back seat, or from the front. It made no difference."[7] Radical openness of this kind was not universal even in the early days, and where it did exist, it soon weakened in the face of pragmatic concerns for efficiency and order. Nevertheless, the remembered or imagined past cast a long shadow, and for decades to come Pentecostalism would provide remarkable opportunities for free sermonizing through "testimony services" and the interpretation of tongues.

PENTECOSTAL PERSUASION

By 1908 the Azusa Street revival had far outstripped Wales and India not only in notoriety but in organizational consequences as well. Unlike them, it became a driving force for a burgeoning new movement. Azusa Street contributed more than its share of recruits to the Pentecostal joint forces whose ranks also included those commissioned by Parham, but more importantly, it lent a symbolic center to an essentially acephalous phenomenon. Azusa Street became the original fixed point in the movement's self-history and helped to create a perception of unity as Pentecostalism rapidly nationalized and internationalized. Such a role was much needed. By April 1907, Apostolic Faith congregations from the movement's two wings dotted North America. By 1909, the movement had achieved "geographical ubiquity."[8] Every region of the United States had a Pentecostal presence, with additional missions planted in 50 nations worldwide.

How and why did the movement spread so swiftly? A complete answer to that question remains elusive, but we can identify important factors. First of all, Pentecostals spread their gospel along the byways with which they were familiar, holding to old alliances and trying first to persuade those they knew best. Stated another way, they spread the news in circles where they themselves were known and held credibility. Furthermore, the speed and efficiency of Holiness communication aided the dissemination of their message. The Holiness press comes first to mind in this respect, and indeed publicists like Bartleman bombarded it with hyperbolic accounts of the revival. But it by no means stood alone. The Holiness habit of urgent itinerancy—the astounding mobility of evangelists, ministers, and laity alike—held equal importance. Radical saints, impassioned by the eschatological portent of their times, immersed themselves in their local Holiness scenes, with the most zealous dropping in on several missions in a given week. Leaders in particular routinely crisscrossed the nation in their earnest determination to stay abreast of God's latest things. In such a climate, word of mouth traveled fast.

But merely spreading the word did not guarantee its acceptance. Pentecostals had somehow to persuade other denizens of this pugnacious, independent-minded world that the Holy Ghost baptism they had proclaimed was not in fact the genuine article and that they should therefore seek another that required the performance of a rather exotic behavior, glossolalia. The new gospel, once again, was a hard sell, but Pentecostals had a few things in their favor. First, the new doctrine neatly matched the norms and expectations of radical Holiness—no surprise since radical Holiness comprised the interpretive matrix that had called it forth. For example, Pentecostalism fused the eschatological and restorationist impulses of Holiness into a powerful narrative that held prima facie plausibility. The most persuasive version of the narrative spun an analogy. Los Angeles was Jerusalem, and Azusa Street the Latter Rain:

> Pentecost has come to Los Angeles, the American Jerusalem. Every sect, creed, and doctrine under Heaven is found in Los Angeles, as well as every nation[,]....sent of God for 'Pentecost'...Surely we are in the days of the restoration, the 'last days,' wonderful days, glorious days.[9]

The Pentecostal construction of Spirit baptism, with glossolalia as a mandatory sign, also solved a technical difficulty. Absent any definitive marker, one's baptism remained subjective, and indeed Holiness saints were known to revise their personal testimonies to accommodate newer and more powerful experiences that might supplant prior anointings as their true baptisms. Glossolalia removed that ambiguity. Naturally, the inherent difficulty of the act raised the price of Holy Ghost baptism, but the higher price purchased a higher degree of certitude.

Apart from this reformulation of Spirit baptism, Pentecostal doctrine at first hewed closely to the line of Holiness orthodoxy. Pentecostals had no quibble with A. B. Simpson's fourfold gospel: Jesus as Savior, Sanctifier, Healer, and Coming King. They merely added Pentecostal baptism as a fifth vital emphasis. In short, Pentecostal logic appealed to Holiness "common sense," drawing on its received proof texts, shared assumptions, common experiences, and accepted standards of evidence while building a case for new exegetical and experiential conclusions. Pentecostalism, that is to say, was an insider alternative, and it fit.

Given the nature of the audience, religious ecstasy formed a vital part of the argument. It was not enough for Pentecostals to apply the literal hermeneutic and utter the rhetorical shibboleths familiar to their hearers, because Holiness epistemology demanded more than logic and rhetoric. It demanded palpable evidence of divine truth. Pentecostalism did not disappoint. At Azusa Street and elsewhere, the faithful heard about, witnessed, personally experienced, and then testified to baptisms of epic proportions, surpassing if possible even the startling ecstasies that had been the stock-in-trade of Irwin and his Fire-Baptized saints. A. J. Tomlinson reported that during his baptism his jaws clamped shut, every limb of his body was "twisted about," he shook, rolled back and forth, and then levitated on a "great sheet of power"—all this while speaking in 10 different languages. William Howard Durham "jerked and quaked...for about three hours." Levi Rakestraw Lupton was struck down for nine.[10]

Some have interpreted Pentecostalism as a revitalization movement, positing a decline in emotionalism within Holiness at approximately the time of its emergence, in which case Pentecostalism would have been to Holiness what Holiness had been to Methodism.[11] Be that as it may, the striking ecstasies manifest in Pentecostal worship played an essential role in its growth not only because they met the psychic and kinetic criteria of Holiness epistemology and thus persuaded others, but also because they persuaded the Pentecostals themselves. Their own certainty, in turn, proved contagious. Pentecostals were convincing because they were themselves convinced.

A final clue to Pentecostalism's extraordinary success lies in the relentless, indefatigable efforts of its apologists. This quality owed much to the uncanny motivational potential of Pentecostal eschatology. Latter Rain millenarianism placed humanity at the brink of the Second Coming, a cataclysmic event that portended both global doom and personal deliverance. But Pentecostals also read in Matthew 24:14 that "this gospel...shall be preached in all the world for a witness unto all nations; and then shall the end come." This seemed to make the Second Coming contingent upon their ability to proclaim the full Gospel around the world. Pentecostal eschatology, then, generated a psychologically complex, even bifurcated mood. The euphoria of the Latter Rain, the tragedy of a dying world, an urgent mandate—"Go ye into all the world, and preach the gospel to every creature"—fused into an anxious triumphalism that underwrote "a frenzy of expansionist activity." No great wonder, then, that Pentecostals rose early, went hungry, and stayed up late in service to their cause. They knew that a righteous God, a Coming King, and perishing souls were counting on them.[12]

As with any outburst of evangelism, most who heard the message did not in fact accept it. The surprising fact is that so many who did found it permanently satisfying. A hefty share of radical Holiness saints could have been called dogmatic seekers—stern advocates of whatever truth they at a given moment happened to hold but likely to pass through several variations on the veritable over time. Pentecostalism proved uniquely capable of slaking that thirst. Perhaps this reflects the degree to which Pentecostalism itself was a product of seeker discontent, fashioned by those who required the most exacting degrees of intensity and the most incontrovertible forms of spiritual proof. Pentecostalism, then, grew partly by self-selection, distinguishing itself as the movement of, by, and for the most restless and demanding saints. Within the ranks of radical Holiness, many fit that description.

However we explain the growth of early Pentecostalism, grow it did, and quite impressively. The pattern at Los Angeles appears to have been typical of both the rate and the mode of Pentecostal expansion. Some congregations, such as James Alexander's Apostolic Faith Mission, sprouted as offshoots of the Azusa Street Mission. Others, including the mission at Eighth and Maple founded by Bartleman and William Pendleton, emerged independently but were influenced or inspired by Azusa. Several Holiness churches split over the new doctrine, with the Pentecostal wing leaving to form its own congregation. Examples here would include Franklin Hill's Vernon Mission and Elmer Fisher's Upper Room Mission (founded by exiles from the Second Pentecostal Church of the Nazarene and Joseph Smale's First New Testament Church, respectively). On occasion, an existing Holiness church converted en masse, as with Arthur Osterberg's Full Gospel Mission. Some congregations, like Durham's Seventh Street Mission, sprang from divisions among the Azusa Street faithful themselves. Finally, new congregations grew out of work among particular ethnic or language groups, such as the Apostolic Mission of Abundio and Rosa de Lopez.

Pentecostalism devastated Holiness bodies large and small. Even older communions like the Free Methodists and the Free Will Baptists suffered major defections or outright breaches. In the minds of Pentecostals, only the devil could make someone oppose this outpouring of the Holy Spirit. In the minds of their Holiness kin, only the devil could make someone accept it. With each side convinced of its own rectitude, the dispute flared into a civil war. Groups like the Pentecostal Church of the Nazarene and the Pentecostal Union dropped "Pentecostal" from their names, and eminent figures like Reuben Torrey and William Godbey bitterly denounced the new movement. Alma White called it "the greatest religious farce that has ever camouflaged under the name of Christianity."[13] Pentecostals struck back, but mainly they just kept moving forward, augmenting the overlapping networks of congregations, sects, enterprises, and associations taking shape across the United States.

EARLY PENTECOSTAL NETWORKS

Although Pentecostalism erupted first in the Midwest and West, its most rapid growth in the United States would ultimately occur in the South. Here, the largest Holiness bodies converted en masse. The single figure most responsible for this turn of events was Gaston Barnabas Cashwell, a 250-pound evangelist from A. B. Crumpler's Holiness Church of North Carolina. Having followed events at Azusa Street avidly through the Holiness press, in November 1906 he hopped a train for Los Angeles to see for himself. His brief sojourn at Azusa Street yielded a fervent Pentecostal baptism and deliverance from "rheumatism and catarrh" to boot.

Cashwell returned to Dunn, North Carolina, in December and on New Year's Eve he commenced a month-long revival that rivaled the wonders of Azusa Street and captured the attention of saints throughout the South. Over the next two years, Cashwell evangelized at a frenetic pace, initiating many of the region's most important Holiness leaders into their personal Pentecosts. The list included Joseph Hillary King, Nickels John Holmes, George Floyd Taylor, Francis Marion Britton, Mack M. Pinson, and A. J. Tomlinson. Through their agency and Cashwell's evangelism, the Holiness Church of North Carolina, the Fire-Baptized Holiness Church, and the Church of God aligned with the new movement.

Ironically, Cashwell himself left the movement in 1909 for an independent ministry, but by then the Pentecostalization of Southern Holiness was virtually complete, the bodies mentioned above having been joined by the Memphis-based Church of God in Christ; the Church of God, Mountain Assembly; the Pentecostal Free Will Baptist Church; and networks associated with Pinson, H. G. Rodgers, and Leonard P. Adams—three evictees from J. O. McClurkan's Pentecostal Mission at Nashville, Tennessee.

A majority of American Pentecostals today reside in the South, but initially the Northern tier more than held its own. Broad-shouldered Chicago, benefiting from the reciprocal efforts of both wings of the early movement, stood as the most important nexus outside of Los Angeles. Parham made the first inroads here, gathering a remnant of Zion that eventually included Marie Burgess, John Lake, Gordon Lindsay, J. Roswell Flower, Daniel C. O. Opperman, and William Hamner Piper along with many others. And after 1906, as Azusa Street rose to the fore, the Chicago–Los Angeles corridor developed into a lively axis of Pentecostal exchange.

Two Chicago congregations bear special mention. The Stone Church, organized in 1906 by Piper and home to future leaders like George C. Brinkman, quickly emerged as a force for missionary outreach and publication in the young movement. Its presses churned out volumes of tracts, books, and pamphlets, along with the *Latter Rain Evangel*, edited by Dowie's former secretary, Anna C. Reiff. The second congregation is William Durham's North Avenue Mission. In 1907 Durham traveled to Azusa Street on the strength of recommendations from colleagues in the Iowa-based World's Faith Missionary Association. The revival he ignited upon his return transformed his congregation into a Pentecostal powerhouse that spawned satellite churches, commissioned foreign missionaries, and brought Pentecost into local immigrant communities. For example, a North Avenue elder, F. A. Sandgren, published *Folke Vennen* as a resource for Swedish, Norwegian, and Danish evangelism, and Durham's mission nurtured both Luigi Francescon's Italian American Assemblea Cristiana of Chicago and the Persian outreach of Andrew Urshan.

As Pentecostalism spread through the Northern Holiness ranks, other regional hubs surfaced to rival Chicago for pride of place. Indianapolis, a major crossroads of radical Holiness and home to such notables as George Eldridge, Thomas Nelson, and Christian Wismer Ruth, now played host to a vibrant Pentecostal scene. Azusa Street emissaries with ties to the city—including Glenn Cook and Seymour himself—met a warm reception among Christian and Missionary Alliance saints like Joseph and Alice Reynolds Flower, and a flourishing interracial movement gathered around Garfield Thomas Haywood, whose dynamic congregation and widely read periodical, *Voice in the Wilderness*, made him one of the movement's preeminent African American leaders.

The slender but potent strain of Quaker Holiness made its contributions to Pentecostalism as well. In Ohio, evangelist Levi Lupton, editor of *The New Acts*, turned his Alliance-based operation into a Pentecostal transit center and clearinghouse; a Pentecostal camp meeting he organized in 1907 drew an interracial crowd of 700 from 21 states and Canada, including some of the movement's most prominent leaders. Elsewhere in Ohio, Thomas King Leonard and William F. Manley established important centers in Findley and Akron, respectively.

In New York, the five Duncan sisters—Elizabeth Baker, Nellie Fell, Mary Work, and Susan and Harriet Duncan—joined the Pentecostal fold, yielding a complex of New York ventures that included Elim Tabernacle, Faith Home, and Publishing House; the Rochester Bible Training School; and *Trust* magazine. Rochester served as an upstate counterpoint to the thriving work in Manhattan established by Marie Burgess (later Burgess-Brown) who had been sent from Zion to New York City by Parham. In New England, Joel Adams Wright's evangelistic association, First Fruits Harvesters, joined the Pentecostal chorus, as did the Christian Workers Union, founded in Springfield, Massachusetts, by Samuel Otis, editor of *Word and Work*. Across the border in Canada, Toronto and Winnipeg emerged as key centers of Pentecostal agitation.

In addition to these explicitly Pentecostal operations, many branches of the Christian and Missionary Alliance functioned as de facto points on the Pentecostal grid. Virginia Moss, founder of what became Beulah Heights Missionary and Training School in North Bergen, New Jersey, experienced Pentecostal baptism at Nyack, New York, and Minnie Draper, one of Simpson's key aides, established Bethel Pentecostal Assembly in Newark. Indeed, a long and storied roster of Pentecostal leaders arrived with Alliance credentials, including one of the movement's best-known theologians and hymnists, D. Wesley Myland. So great was the Pentecostal influence that Simpson reorganized his association in 1912 to prevent further predations.

Like the Deep South and the Northern tier of states, the Southwest and the Southern plains gave rise to several notable Pentecostal hubs, including "Mother" Mary Moise's faith home in St. Louis; Albert S. Copley's Grace and Glory ministry in Kansas City; and Malvern, Arkansas, where E. N. Bell published the influential *Word and Witness*. But Parham's Apostolic Faith Movement remained the region's most extensive Pentecostal network. Unfortunately, it was also the first to be hit by personal scandal.

In July 1907, Parham was detained in San Antonio, Texas, in the company of a young man and charged with sodomy. What actually transpired on that hot summer night may never be known, but Parham's standing suffered irreparable harm, notwithstanding the fact that charges were later dropped. News of the scandal shot through Holiness and Pentecostal circles, delighting Parham's enemies and disheartening his dwindling cadre of friends. Meanwhile, the Apostolic Faith Movement shattered. Parham's leading associates, Howard Goss and W. Faye Carothers, discharged the Projector from his post and took command of as much of the organization as they could gather. Parham, for his part, adamantly denied any wrongdoing and retained the loyalty of several thousand followers. Relocating to Baxter Springs, Kansas, he continued to publish the *Apostolic Faith* and to oversee his small branch of the Pentecostal movement.

Out West, the multiplying missions of greater Los Angeles, which now included Finis Yoakum's Pisgah Home and Gardens, merged into an expanding web of regional centers. The San Francisco Bay area featured Robert and Mary Craig's Glad Tidings Temple and, after 1908, a complex of concerns tied to Holiness celebrity Carrie Judd Montgomery that included the Home of Peace missionary retreat, a missionary training center, the World-Wide Pentecostal Camp Meeting, and the highly regarded *Triumphs of Faith*. Like Moss and Draper, Montgomery was a close associate of Simpson, and she and her husband George brought wealth, international renown, and an air of respectability to their new affiliation. Elsewhere, Pentecostal outposts sprang up in places like Spokane and Seattle, Washington, and in Denver, Colorado, where one of the movement's most scathing critics, Alma White, had her Pentecostal Union shaken and her family divided by the defection of her husband, Kent, to Pentecostalism.

Meanwhile, the West Coast wing of the Apostolic Faith suffered its own division when Florence Crawford, whom Seymour had designated as his state director in 1906, ventured out on her own. Seymour had relied on Crawford not only for her personal talents but also for her ties to important patrons like William C. Trotter, former superintendent of the Union Rescue Mission in Los Angeles and a friend of oil magnate Lyman Stewart. In late 1907, however, Crawford relocated to Portland, where she organized an independent branch of the Apostolic Faith that encompassed several congregations originally formed under the influence of Azusa Street. Trotter promptly joined her in Portland, and Clara Lum, Seymour's personal secretary and editor of the *Apostolic Faith*, soon followed. To make matters worse for Seymour, Lum saw the paper as her own, so she took it and its mailing list with her. Henceforth, the *Apostolic Faith* would radiate from Portland and in service to Crawford's organization.

The regional emphasis developed above should not be pressed. Well-traveled pathways connected the various sectors of the movement, and itinerant evangelists, short-term Bible schools, annual camp meetings, periodicals, and the general practice of visitation fostered brisk interaction and a sense of common purpose across a broad spectrum of Pentecostalism. But the era of solidarity, such as it was, proved fleeting.

A COMMON FAITH

The pinnacle of Pentecostal accord came early and passed quickly. Despite the tremors that shook each wing of the Apostolic Faith Movement, the period prior to 1910 stands out in hindsight for its relative amity. When Cashwell launched the *Bridegroom's Messenger* in 1907, for example, he assembled a pan-Pentecostal board of contributing editors that included A. J. Tomlinson (Church of God), H. H. Goff (Free-Will Baptist), N. J. Holmes (Holiness Presbyterian), R. B. Hayes (Fire-Baptized Holiness), M. M. Pinson (Pentecostal Mission), and members of his own denomination like G. F. Taylor and A. H. Butler. The content of his paper, moreover, matched the ecumenical tone of his board, featuring articles such as "Unity of the Faith" that cast Pentecostalism as a cure for the "schisms and isms" plaguing Christendom.

This unity was not entirely illusory, and it is particularly striking to note how quickly Pentecostalism achieved self-consciousness as a single, coherent phenomenon. Parham and his followers almost immediately framed their experience not as a serviceable enhancement of the old Holiness gospel but as the first full restoration of the Apostolic Faith. Even as Parham's work faded into the shadow of Azusa Street, that basic self-conception persisted. One year after Azusa Street, pioneering evangelist Ivey Campbell of Ohio penned an article for Lupton's *New Acts* entitled, "April Ninth, 1907: Anniversary Day for the 20th Century Pentecostal Movement." The following year, W. F. Carothers, Parham's former associate and now successor, published a "History of Movement."[14] As Cashwell's 1909 exit from the movement made clear, however, fraternity had its limits. Pentecostal commonalities proved to be no match for real and imagined differences, partly because the differences were amplified by a widely shared independent streak. Indeed, it is tempting to say that a common faith was doomed by a common personality trait.

Rugged individualism in matters of belief seemed to be hard-wired into the saints, along with an "iron-fisted determination always to speak one's mind, regardless of the human cost."[15] Most Pentecostals, furthermore, espoused an ecclesiology that matched their temperament, rejecting anything that smacked of hierarchy in favor of the rule of the Holy Spirit, the rights of the congregation, and individual liberty of conscience. Even those more favorably inclined to organization applied it with a light touch, as when Parham's regional directors disclaimed "authority over any branch of the work" and left seasoned evangelists "free to direct their own movements, subject only to the bonds of love and unity."[16]

Temperament and ecclesiology, of course, only partly explain the dissension that rocked Pentecostalism in its second decade. Like Holiness, it had gathered members from many theological points of origin but lacked the dominant institutions or universally accepted leadership capable of unifying them. Under those circumstances, prospects for a uniform interpretation of the one tangible authority all Pentecostals did agree on—the Bible—were slim, indeed.

SCHISM, IF YOU COULD CALL IT THAT

Given its acephalous nature, perhaps we should not call what happened to early Pentecostalism in its second decade schism. The movement had no formal structure to split from, no codified orthodoxy to deviate from. That being said, its original vision of unity barely made it past infancy, and by 1916 Pentecostalism had fractured into a threefold division that persists to this day.

The first general controversy to trouble the Pentecostal waters swirled around the central Holiness tenet of entire sanctification. Many Reformed or Higher Life adherents had never fully accepted the Wesleyan formulation, which defined sanctification as a crisis experience subsequent to conversion that totally eradicated one's sinful nature. These saints found an able voice in William Durham. Durham placed sanctification within the framework of the Finished Work of Calvary—terminology used by his former associates in the World's Faith Missionary Association and by the well-known evangelist and educator, Essek William Kenyon. This perspective framed sanctification as the power to live a holy life set apart for God's service and included it within the full salvation purchased for believers by Christ on the cross. Furthermore, believers were said to appropriate sanctification progressively, through faith as enabled by the Holy Spirit, not instantaneously through a second work of grace. The result was a doctrine of sanctification much closer to that held by the majority of American Christians.

Throughout 1910 Durham aggressively advanced his Finished Work views, trumpeting the doctrine in the pages of his journal, the *Pentecostal Testimony,* and barnstorming stops on the Pentecostal circuit like Bell's Malvern, Arkansas, headquarters and Burgess-Brown's Glad Tidings Temple in New York City. Meanwhile, a growing number of eager surrogates sallied forth on his behalf. Not surprisingly, the Finished Work met its warmest embrace among Pentecostals of Presbyterian, Baptist, Alliance, and other non-Wesleyan extraction.

In February 1911, Durham took his battle to the symbolic heart of early Pentecostalism: the Azusa Street Mission. With Seymour out of town, he commandeered the now declining mission and sparked a revival reminiscent of Azusa's heyday. For the next two months the historic mission served as a base of operations from which Durham and his coworkers launched apologetic forays up and down the West Coast. When Seymour returned in April and demanded his pulpit, however, matters came to a head. Durham appealed to his popularity with the congregants and refused to comply. Seymour and the trustees appealed to their legal authority and locked him out of the mission. Ousted from Azusa Street, Durham opened a competing assembly nearby that attracted hundreds of attendees and provided a new locus for the promotion of Finished Work teaching throughout the United States and Canada.

The dispute over sanctification quickly turned bitter. Defenders of the original formula, led by Parham, Seymour, Crawford, and most Southern Pentecostal leaders, excoriated Durham and his "damnable doctrine," opposing both at every turn. Early in 1912, Parham struck an Old Testament pose and prayed God to smite dead either himself or Durham, whoever the false prophet might be. When Durham fell to tuberculosis six months later at the age of 39, Parham heralded his death as divine vindication of the Holiness Pentecostal cause. Durham's death, however, did little to dampen enthusiasm for the doctrine he had proclaimed. A permanent breach had opened between those who held to the original Wesleyan-Holiness formula and those who viewed sanctification as an aspect of full salvation progressively realized through faith and the work of the Holy Spirit.[17]

The battlefield still lay heavy with the smell of spent invective when a second and yet more acrimonious conflict erupted over a fundamental tenet of Christian orthodoxy. Primarily contained within the Finished Work camp, it was known as the New Issue and called the triune nature of God into question. The controversy surfaced, ironically, at the 1913 Apostolic Faith World Wide Camp Meeting, a celebration of Pentecostal unity that reprised the original Azusa Street camp meetings of 1907 and 1908, held like them in the Arroyo Seco and organized by the same former Seymour aide, Robert Scott. But in a telling sign of how dramatically things had changed since 1908, Seymour himself played virtually no role in the meetings while famed evangelist Maria Woodworth-Etter, having cast her lot with the movement the year before, arrived as the keynote speaker.

The New Issue blossomed from a narrow debate over which baptismal formula a proper Apostolic Church should employ. As noted, dogmatism and literalism ran deep in the Pentecostal bloodlines, and many felt a certain urgency about getting the matter exactly right. Against that backdrop, Canadian pastor and Azusa veteran Robert Edward McAlister delivered a sermon in which he argued that a close study of the New Testament proved that the apostles had always used some variant of Acts 2:38 ("in the name of Jesus Christ") as opposed to the Trinitarian formula given in Matthew 28:19 ("in the name of the Father, and of the Son, and of the Holy Ghost"). Early the next morning his sermon won dramatic punctuation from a fellow camper who reported a direct revelation from the Holy Spirit confirming McAlister's conclusion.

Contrary to what one might gather from their emphasis on Spirit baptism and charismatic gifts, Pentecostals in fact practiced a profoundly Jesus-centered piety, which made baptism "in Jesus' name" quite appealing. For most, the issue never evolved beyond an earnest effort to find the correct baptismal formula. For others, however, it opened into a sweeping reconsideration of the nature of God.

One such person was Australian-born evangelist Frank Ewart, William Durham's former associate and now successor at Seventh Street Mission. As Ewart pondered the deeper implications of this apparently innocuous baptismal alteration, the mystery of the Godhead flared forth in an epiphany that neatly reconciled Acts 2:38 and Matthew 28:19. "Jesus," Ewart realized, *was* the name of the Father, the Son, and the Holy Ghost. The three were in fact one God, in one person, with one name.

In 1914, Ewart went public with his astonishing insight into the oneness of God, working in tandem with Glenn Cook, Seymour's old right-hand man. Cook proved to be no less persuasive an advocate for this doctrinal reform than he had been for the original Pentecostal message, bearing witness to Jesus' name in places like St. Louis and his old hometown of Indianapolis, where he rebaptized G. T. Haywood. Through the combined efforts of Cook and Haywood, Indianapolis emerged as perhaps the premier center of Oneness Pentecostalism in the United States. Over the next few years, thousands of Pentecostals, including notables like Howard Goss, D.C.O. Opperman, and Andrew Urshan joined the Oneness cause, and a new theological gash—the deepest and most intractable of all—cut across the surface of the young movement.

Meanwhile, back in the staunchly Wesleyan-Holiness South, a less severe but still enduring rift opened not over the nature of God, but over the nature of God's church. By 1909, the Church of God had arrived at a unique blend of episcopal and Landmark Baptist ecclesiology, largely under the influence of its two most prominent leaders, A. J. Tomlinson and Richard Spurling. The most controversial feature of this hybrid lay in its exclusivist doctrine of the Visible Church. The church as defined in the New Testament, they argued, denoted neither a vague spiritual unity of all believers nor an invisible ecclesia mysteriously present in each local congregation, but rather a literal institution commissioned by the Holy Spirit on the Day of Pentecost. Only those who had been properly received into a duly-ordained branch of that institution could truly be considered members of the Body of Christ. And that institution, in its latter-day apparition, happened to be the Church of God with headquarters in Cleveland, Tennessee.

Other Southern saints were quick to rebut these notions. "They call it the 'Church of God,'" fumed F. M. Britton, "and say that they are right and all others are wrong." Britton begged to differ. "Every child of God is in the church of God," he declared. "We enter in through the blood of the everlasting covenant."[18] The divide separating the Church of God from other Pentecostals never yawned so widely as did the chasms formed by the two great issues described above, but like them it persisted as a vivid reminder both of the movement's richness and diversity and of the daunting obstacles to unity within it.

THE THREE BRANCHES OF
CLASSICAL PENTECOSTALISM

By 1915, the basic contours of classical Pentecostalism had been set. The wellspring of a common faith would henceforth flow through three basic tributaries: Holiness, Reformed or Finished Work, and Oneness. Each of these could be (and would be) further subdivided along regional, racial, cultural, doctrinal, and liturgical lines, but future tempests would play out largely within the confines of a single branch of a triform movement.

The intra-Pentecostal polemic that fractured the movement also drove it sharply toward formal organization, as theological difference took institutional form. Most early adherents, as we have seen, were spiritual libertarians who spurned ecclesiasticism. The South, where organized Holiness sects had been the norm prior to the rise of Pentecostalism, presented something of an exception to the rule, but even there radical congregationalism often inflected the meaning of organization. As late as 1915, Martin L. Ryan boasted that Pentecostalism "has no great earthly leader. It is not a religious organization. It will not be organized."[19] By the time Ryan penned those words, however, the travail of disputation had already begun to overwhelm the primitivist impulse he expressed.

The shock and awe of theological warfare, then, supplied the most convincing argument for the benefits of organization. But other considerations also weighed in its favor. Coordinated, collective action promised greater efficiency in the application of resources, greater regularity of standards, and greater control over what was done in the name of one's brand of Pentecostalism. These prospects held special attraction for the growing number of Pentecostals who by the early 1910s wished to temper the intense emotionalism that pervaded (and to their minds discredited) the movement.[20]

Because the aversion to organization voiced by Ryan had been a virtual consensus outside the South, steps in that direction had to be finessed in a way that reconciled past idealism with present felt needs, and without giving the appearance that the movement had ventured onto a slippery slope toward the very denominationalism it had so often and so categorically condemned. The solution was to construe the process as mere *association*—a term unencumbered by the negative connotations attached to *organization*—and to forswear restrictive accoutrements like creeds and hierarchy. Once that door was open, a flurry of institution building ensued that by 1918 had produced most of today's largest Pentecostal denominations.

The oldest bodies had already emerged, as noted, in the South. All sprang from Holiness sects that had joined the Pentecostal movement in the years immediately following the Azusa Street revival, and together they formed the core of the Holiness wing of the movement. The most important from a historical perspective were the Big Three of Southern Pentecostalism: the Church of God (Cleveland, Tennessee), the Church of God in Christ, and the Pentecostal Holiness Church.

The Church of God grew from a small network of Holiness believers in eastern Tennessee and western North Carolina affiliated with Richard G. Spurling, Jr., and William F. Bryant. In 1902 the group organized as the Holiness Church at Camp Creek, North Carolina. The following year, it acquired the services of A. J. Tomlinson, an Indiana-born ex-Quaker who had attempted to found a Holiness compound nearby modeled after Sandford's commune at Shiloh. A charismatic and visionary figure, Tomlinson dominated the sect for the next 20 years. Under his leadership, the group relocated its headquarters to Cleveland, Tennessee, and changed its name to the Church of God. By early 1909, it had moved solidly into the Pentecostal camp, though, as we have seen, it distinguished itself from other Pentecostal bodies by adopting an exclusivist ecclesiology.

At the other end of the state, the similarly named Church of God in Christ flourished from its base in Memphis, Tennessee. Formed in 1897 by C. H. Mason and C. P. Jones, the denomination claimed as many as 60 congregations in six states when Mason received Holy Ghost baptism during a 1906 trip to Los Angeles. The following year Mason and Jones fell out over the new doctrine, with Mason carrying the church name and approximately half of its congregations into Pentecostalism. Though predominantly African American, the Church of God in Christ embraced the ideal of interracial membership, and Mason shared the privileges of his legally incorporated body with unaffiliated white ministers, granting credentials that allowed them to perform weddings and enjoy reduced rail fares.

The last of the Southern Big Three grew from a merger of three Holiness bodies that had joined the Pentecostal movement in the same wave of Cashwell-inspired revivalism that had transformed the

Church of God. The oldest was B. H. Irwin's Fire-Baptized Holiness Church, founded in 1895 and headquartered after 1898 in Anderson, South Carolina. The organization had almost collapsed in 1900, when an unspecified moral infraction prompted Irwin's abrupt resignation. Under the leadership of J. H. King, however, it survived and had recouped many of its Southern losses by the time it endorsed Pentecostalism in 1908.

The Holiness Church of North Carolina, Cashwell's old body, formed a second partner in the merger. Founded by A. B. Crumpler in 1900, virtually all of its ministers accepted Pentecostalism on the strength of Cashwell's testimony. Crumpler himself held out, but when Cashwell and George F. Taylor led a Pentecostal takeover in 1908, Crumpler resigned, opening the way to a full embrace of the new movement. The following year, the group changed its name to the Pentecostal Holiness Church. Finally, the Tabernacle Pentecostal Church, a group of congregations affiliated with N. J. Holmes's ministry and Bible school near Greenville, South Carolina, rounded out the partnership.

Following their Pentecostalization, these three groups interacted frequently and found that they shared similar views and had common interests, including rivalry with the Church of God. In 1911, after two years of negotiation, the Fire-Baptized Holiness Church and the Pentecostal Holiness Church merged under the name of the latter. Four years later, the Tabernacle Pentecostal Church joined the new denomination, although Holmes Bible and Missionary Institute retained its independence.

Outside the South, Crawford's Apostolic Faith Mission stood as the best known representative of the Holiness-Pentecostal option. Its mother church in Portland oversaw an expanding network of satellite congregations that together claimed several thousand members. Other important Holiness-Pentecostal denominations included the African American Fire-Baptized Holiness Church, which had separated from the white body in 1908 under the leadership of William E. Fuller; the Camp Fear, Wilmington, New River, and South Carolina conferences of the Free-Will Baptist Church; the Pentecostal Fire-Baptized Holiness Church, which split from the newly formed Pentecostal Holiness Church in 1916; and the Holy Church of North Carolina and Virginia, incorporated in 1918 as the United Holy Church of America.

Southern Pentecostalism stood out from its regional peers for its emphasis on sanctification, its ethical rigorism, and its strict church discipline. In addition, the Pentecostal tendencies toward literalism and emotional intensity received their fullest expression here. For example, the region gave birth to the phenomenon of serpent handling, a Pentecostal subculture that, though marginal, has etched one of the movement's most enduring popular images. Tracing to the ministry of Church of God evangelist George W. Hensley, serpent handlers measured their authenticity by the standard of Mark 16:17–18: "And these signs shall follow them that believe; In my name shall they cast out devils; they shall speak with new tongues; They shall take up serpents; and if they drink any deadly thing, it shall not hurt them." Leaders like Tomlinson were slow to condemn the practice because of its textual basis and its apparent validation of their claim that all of the apostolic signs and wonders had been restored among them. Condemnation would eventually come, but only after serpent handling had gone unchecked for several years.

Finished Work Pentecostals lagged behind their Holiness peers in the business of organization, both because they emerged late as a self-conscious group and because their ranks included some of the staunchest foes of ecclesiasticism. But organize they did when E. N. Bell, Howard Goss, Daniel Opperman, Archibald Collins, and Mack Pinson convened a General Council of Pentecostal leaders at Hot Springs, Arkansas, in April 1914.

Those who gathered "to co-operate in love and peace" at Hot Springs came primarily from four or five overlapping networks. These included the share of the Midwestern Apostolic Faith that had not remained loyal to Parham; Southern white Pentecostal ministers affiliated with Goss, Pinson, H. G. Rodgers, and L. P. Adams (many of whom had been credentialed by Mason); a greater Chicago circle of ministers, many with ties to Durham's North Avenue Mission or William Piper's Stone Church and often former Dowieites; and converts from Christian and Missionary Alliance or Elim circles. The organization they formed, the Assemblies of God, quickly developed into the nation's largest Pentecostal denomination in terms of membership and breadth of geographic distribution, aided by future acquisitions such as its 1917 absorption of the Holiness Baptist Churches of Southwestern Arkansas.

As if to prove it had no designs on denominationalism, the Assemblies of God left Hot Springs with neither constitution nor creed. But sanguine hopes for unity as a fruit of the Spirit rather than of ecclesiastical coercion broke on the stone of the New Issue. The Assemblies of God seemed willing to tolerate a degree of variation on the point of sanctification, though the process of self-selection had rendered the sentiment rather moot since an overwhelming majority shared the Finished Work position. But Oneness doctrine—held to or sympathized with by a significant minority of the new body—carried liberty a bridge too far for the Trinitarian majority.

In 1916, the General Council of the Assemblies of God passed a Statement of Fundamental Truths that explicitly affirmed the doctrine of the Trinity. To the eyes of critics it also explicitly betrayed a 1914 promise not to "legislate...laws and articles of faith." During the subsequent fallout, a Oneness exodus combined with the departure of antidenominational affiliates like executive presbyter John Chalmers Sinclair to trim the roster of perhaps a quarter of its membership.

In the months following the purge, Daniel Opperman, a cosponsor of the Hot Springs council and the most prominent Oneness defector, gathered fellow refugees into a General Assembly of Apostolic Assemblies, based in Eureka Springs, Arkansas. Meanwhile, G. T. Haywood had already led the majority of the Pentecostal Assemblies of the World—a loose federation of saints founded in 1907 by J. J. Frazee—into the Oneness fold. In 1918 Opperman's Assemblies were absorbed into the Pentecostal Assemblies of the World, which legally incorporated under that name in Indianapolis the following year. Meanwhile, two additional Oneness bodies took shape: the Asamblea Apostólica de la Fe en Cristo Jesús (Apostolic Assembly of Faith in Christ Jesus), founded by Azusa Street converts Luis Lopez and Juan Navarro; and a rare Holiness variant, the predominantly black Apostolic Overcoming Holy Church of God, founded by William T. Phillips in Mobile, Alabama, in 1917.

For all three branches of Pentecostalism, the advantages of organization proved readily apparent as nascent denominations of every type experienced rapid growth and increased professionalism. Tomlinson's Church of God, for example, counted 31 churches and 1,000 members in six states in 1910. By 1917 it had grown tenfold, to more than 300 churches and 10,000 members spread over 20 states and the Caribbean. Organized Pentecostalism would never be the whole story, and especially in the early years many resisted the yoke of affiliation. But from the second decade of the 20th century forward, Pentecostal institutions provided the driving force of the movement.

Despite the marking of territory and the building of walls, lively commerce persisted across Pentecostalism, and not only among the unaligned. Here, the movement's evangelists led the way. The most celebrated of these was Woodworth-Etter, the matriarch of mass evangelism, but the number included Carrie Montgomery, Fred Francis Bosworth, and storied British evangelist Smith Wigglesworth. Partly because an ecumenical posture served their promotional interests, these men and women helped keep channels of communication and mutual influence open even as the movement began to balkanize.

Meanwhile, a new generation of evangelists began its rise to the stage. Leading the way was a charismatic young Canadian by the name of Aimee Semple McPherson, who knew how to tell a story and spellbind a crowd. In her ministry, modern styles, values, and technology would mix with traditional religion in paradoxical and unpredictable ways, and she, more than any other, would break the old mold and fashion a new one for those who came after.

Looking back from the vantage point of the late 1910s, it is rather astonishing to consider what had occurred in such a short span of time. A movement had emerged, expanded, and subdivided, spawning a score of organizations with hundreds of congregations claiming tens of thousands of adherents in the United States and abroad. It had also provoked a host of enemies who lashed out at the movement or predicted its rapid demise. Scornful critics like Holiness theologian Harry A. Ironside—a name made for polemic if ever there was one—derided the "present disgusting 'Tongues Movement'" for its "pandemoniums...worthy of a madhouse or of a collection of howling dervishes."[21] More hopeful adversaries dismissed Pentecostalism as an ephemeral fanaticism that would vanish like mist before the rising sun.

Fanatical it may have been, but ephemeral it surely was not. Pentecostalism was here to stay. That being said, its future remained uncertain. Just ahead lay existential challenges—a global war, a cultural revolution, a wrenching economic depression, a second and greater war—that would test its mettle and determine the kind of movement it was to become.

NOTES

1. My account of Parham depends on James Goff, Jr., *Fields White unto Harvest: Charles F. Parham and the Missionary Origins of Pentecostalism* (Fayetteville: University of Arkansas Press, 1988). Parham on Irwin is from *Apostolic Faith,* April 1925, 3, quoted in Grant Wacker, *Heaven Below: Early Pentecostals and American Culture* (Cambridge, MA: Harvard University Press, 2001), 1. For Parham's adoption of Irwin's Fire-Baptized doctrine, see Randall Stephens, *The Fire Spreads: Holiness and Pentecostalism in the American South* (Cambridge, MA: Harvard University Press, 2008), 188.

2. On Dowie, see Grant Wacker, Chris Armstrong, and Jay S. F. Blossom, "John Alexander Dowie: Harbinger of Pentecostal Power,"

in *Portraits of a Generation: Early Pentecostal Leaders,* eds. James Goff, Jr., and Grant Wacker (Fayetteville: University of Arkansas Press, 2002), 2–19; for Sandford, see Shirley Nelson, *Fair, Clear, and Terrible: The Story of Shiloh, Maine* (Latham, NY: British American Publications, 1989).

3. W. Mallis, "Progress of the Revival in India," *Holiness Advocate,* May 15, 1906, 8.

4. Frank Bartleman, *How Pentecost Came to Los Angeles* (Los Angeles: Frank Bartleman, 1925), 39.

5. My account relies on Cecil M. Robeck, Jr., *The Azusa Street Mission and Revival* (Nashville, TN: Thomas Nelson, 2006), 4–7, 39–60.

6. Ambrose Jessup Tomlinson, Manuscript Diary, Vol. 2, entry for June 16, 1909.

7. Bartleman, *How Pentecost Came,* 59.

8. See Wacker, *Heaven Below,* 212.

9. Bartleman, *How Pentecost Came,* 63–64.

10. Tomlinson, Diary, Vol. 2, entry for January 13, 1908; Durham, report in *Apostolic Faith,* February/March 1907, 4; Lupton, report in *New Acts,* 3, no. 1, February 1907, 3.

11. Stephens, *The Fire Spreads,* 223.

12. Wacker, *Heaven Below,* 251, 31.

13. Susan C. Stanley, "Alma White: The Politics of Dissent," in *Portraits,* 62.

14. Ivey Campbell, "April Ninth, 1907," *New Acts,* June 1907, 9; W. F. Carothers, "History of Movement," *Apostolic Faith* (Houston, Texas), October 1908, 1.

15. Wacker, *Heaven Below,* chap. 1, 78.

16. *Apostolic Faith* (Houston, Texas), October 1908, 7.

17. My treatment of this controversy draws on Robeck, *Azusa Street Mission;* and Edith Blumhofer, "William H. Durham: Years of Creativity, Years of Dissent," in *Portraits,* 123–142.

18. F. M. Britton, "Brother F. M. Britton's Letter," *Apostolic Evangel,* ca. January 1910, 7.

19. M. L. Ryan, in the *Chinese Recorder,* May 1915, 323, quoted in Wacker, *Heaven Below,* 142.

20. See Wacker, *Heaven Below,* 106–107.

21. Harry A. Ironside, *Holiness: The False and the True* (New York: Loizeaux Brothers, 1912), 39.

CHAPTER 3

Pentecost and the World at War

In 1914, as American Pentecostalism fractured under the weight of doctrinal controversy, the Rube Goldberg machine of alliances that Europeans had relied on to skirt disaster collapsed into a maelstrom of war. It was the quintessential modern event, and much of the remaining world was soon pulled into the vortex of what came to be known as the Great War. The world's first truly global conflict catalyzed and accelerated social, economic, and political transformations that would revolutionize life for future generations everywhere. But it proved to be only the foreshock of a yet deadlier and more fully global conflict to erupt a short generation later.

Within this fraught context, Pentecostalism faced the existential imperative of defining itself and its relation to the outside world. Internally, it continued the process described in the previous chapter, forging a set of identities through subdivision and competition. Insiders and outsiders alike tend to view schism as an unmitigated tragedy, and indeed the personal and material costs can be quite high. But religious differentiation is also a mode of clarification and can be a powerful impetus to growth, as indeed it was for Pentecostalism. Externally, the Great War forced the movement's hand, advancing the negotiations whereby Pentecostalism defined its relation to the United States at large and to its rivals, enemies, and peers in the greater world of evangelicalism.

Pentecostalism was a bumptious, contrarian movement with sectarian instincts. Pride, purity, and proof-texts dictated "separation from the world." But an extroverted, missionary-minded movement like Pentecostalism could never be truly separate from the world it defined itself over against yet lived within and sought to save. Now, the fervent nationalism of a nation at war raised the stakes on its trademark nonconformity. As Pentecostalism moved into its second generation, then, it ran headlong into national events that crystallized issues, posed dilemmas, and demanded choices.

PENTECOST AND POLITICS

Religious culture complicated these dilemmas, since most Pentecostals filtered the transcendent events of the early 20th century through an apolitical, dispensationalist lens. To say that early Pentecostals were apolitical is not to say that they had no views on the political questions of their day. But they read the headlines as detached observers who measured the meaning and salience of events by their possible relation to the drama of divine history. Furthermore, they assessed those events through the grid of their own distinctive understanding of humanity's ills. The remedy for those ills, to Pentecostals at the brink of the Second Coming, rarely involved secular politics.

As an interracial movement that empowered women and drew disproportionately from the working poor and the lower middle class, Pentecostalism held abundant political potential. In fact, the saints lashed the crimes of the rich and vices of the poor in language that was dense with political implication. Stray rhetoric notwithstanding, however, the faithful engaged in actual partisan politics rarely and primarily in those cases where politics and morality overlapped, as with Prohibition. Even then, engagement came most often in the form of moral support, not concrete political action, and was laced with eschatological calculations, as when saints decried unions and the ecumenical movement for being stepping stones to the one-world government prophesied in the book of Revelation.

For all intents and purposes, then, most converts turned their back on secular politics when they joined the movement. To the Pentecostal mind, this was merely common sense. Sin and Satan lay at the root of the world's dilemmas, and only personal salvation for the individual and divine intervention for humanity would suffice. Political action, therefore, squandered scarce resources on superficial solutions to misdiagnosed problems.

The conversion of A. J. Tomlinson lends a case in point. Born to a prosperous and politically active family, he seemed destined to follow the family tradition. In 1892, at the age of 27, Tomlinson ran for county office under the banner of the Populist Party, and although he lost that election, a future in politics seemed open to the talented young man. Then, everything changed. He experienced entire sanctification and plunged wholeheartedly into the Holiness movement. From that point forward, he had no use for political endeavors. "My interest in politics vanished so rapidly," Tomlinson explained, "that I was almost surprised." Family and friends urged him to vote and thus to fulfill his patriotic duty, but he refused. "No," he insisted, "I will only vote for Jesus." Looking back from the height of his Pentecostal ministry, he was happy to say, "I never have taken any part in politics since, nor gone to the polls and cast a ballot."[1] For Tomlinson, as for the great majority of his Pentecostal cohorts, politics occurred on the far side of the church-world divide.

The Great War and the New Era that followed, however, disturbed the sectarian peace. They brought intrusive policies like military conscription, War Bond drives, 100 percent Americanism, the Espionage and Sedition Acts, and threatening cultural phenomena like the "New Morality" and the spread of Darwinism. One's response to these worldly matters might still be inflected by dispensationalism, but pragmatic, everyday engagement could not be avoided. Everywhere they turned the saints met pressure to advance or oppose the issues that gripped their fellow citizens. More specifically, they were pressed to define the *nature* of their prophetic voice. Would it be universalistic or nationalistic? Could the heavenly citizen also wave a worldly flag? Would the United States be judged with the other nations, or was it somehow a nation apart? And what were the implications of Pentecostalism for military service? The moral perils of the postwar years likewise challenged the movement's sectarian instincts. What did separation from the world really mean? Should Pentecostals live as pilgrims passing through a world of sin? Or did these new social perils demand more? Should they instead rise up to defend a beleaguered society, alongside their fundamentalist kin?

PENTECOSTALISM AND THE GREAT WAR

One of the great ironies of early Pentecostalism was that its rhetorical and attitudinal militancy usually accompanied an absolute rejection of physical violence. In 1914, that pacifism collided with the realities of a world at war. Pentecostalism had blossomed into an international movement by the time the Guns of August erupted, and American Pentecostals could hardly ignore events threatening their colleagues

abroad. But precisely how they would respond remained an open
question. In the end, a variety of factors conspired to produce a deeply
ambivalent but uniquely Pentecostal response to the Great War on this
side of the Atlantic. Some of these factors steered Pentecostals toward
an antiwar stance similar to that of the pacifist wing of the Progressive
movement. Others undercut that stance and moved Pentecostals back
toward an increasingly jingoistic mainstream.

The foundation of Pentecostal pacifism lay in the movement's literal hermeneutic. Pentecostals were strict biblicists who took New
Testament passages about nonresistance at face value and attempted
to obey them—a habit strengthened by the disproportionate influence of ex-Quakers among them. The movement's populist social
assumptions, moreover, reinforced its pacifist interpretation of the
Bible, predisposing Pentecostals to regard the European affair as a
"rich man's war, poor man's fight."

The dispensationalist paradigm, however, added twists that set
Pentecostals apart from mainstream pacifists in the Progressive Era.
For one thing, dispensationalism encouraged a certain apocalyptic detachment; the war unfolded less as a historical event or moral
dilemma than as a grand cosmic metaphor. For that reason, American
Pentecostals first saw the European war both as a lurid illustration
of spiritual warfare and divine judgment, and as an incontrovertible
sign of the times—proof positive that the rapture was nigh at hand.
In addition, dispensationalism accentuated the universalistic side of
Christian theology and added practical grounds for noninvolvement
to the political implications of one's heavenly citizenship. Charles
Parham had long warned of a "coming struggle" in which "the gov-
ernments, the rich, and the churches" would array against "the new
order that rises out of the sea of humanity," which knew no "national
boundaries" and espoused "the universal brotherhood of mankind."
When the Great War came, then, he found it hard to fathom how those
who believed in Christ's soon return could "fight for the perpetuation
of these nations, which we know will fall as the Gentile age will close
and the millennium come."[2]

These three factors—biblical pacifism, populism, and dispensationalism—were partly offset by three others that gained force as the
war progressed and U.S. involvement neared. First, the evangelical
imperative upheld "winning souls" as the Christian's highest priority.
The war, in turn, promised a harvest of souls among both the troops
and the general populations of war-torn nations. Consequently, a
Pentecostal consensus quickly gathered around the wisdom of seiz-
ing the moment through participation in chaplaincy programs and

missionary outreach to soldiers. Second, as war fever kindled within the United States, concern for the movement's reputation prompted leaders of its major denominations to moderate their stance. Only by demonstrating its patriotism, loyalty, and honor, they felt, could the movement maintain its credibility within the larger society it hoped to win for Christ. Finally, the sheer diversity of the movement—not to mention its lack of strong central authorities—meant that its pacifist leanings would be difficult to articulate consistently or sustain over the long haul. Prominent dissenters existed from the very beginning, and even those who shared the pacifist persuasion reached that destination along somewhat different pathways.

The fluctuating response to the war in the pages of the *Evangel,* the official organ of the newly formed Assemblies of God (AG), illustrates that of the movement at large. The first reference to the war came a short month after its outbreak and placed the conflict firmly within a dispensationalist framework. It was, wrote E. N. Bell, general superintendent of the AG and co-editor of the *Evangel,* "The Second Coming War." As the war stretched on, however, correspondence with European Pentecostals brought it out of the realm of metaphor and into the realm of Christian ethics. So it was that in December 1914, the *Evangel* reprinted a set of editorials by European Pentecostals under the heading, "Is European War Justifiable?" The editorials had first appeared in Anglican rector Alexander Alfred Boddy's influential Pentecostal journal, *Confidence,* and they largely endorsed the Allied cause.

The outcry must have been considerable, because the following month the *Evangel* felt compelled to defend its publication of the pro-war editorials, noting that it was easy for Americans, far removed from the hostilities, to say what should be done, quite another for those on the scene "to find the right thing to do under the circumstances." Then, they balanced the slate by printing a sharply worded reply from Texan Burt McCafferty. "Shall Christians Go to War?" he asked. For McCafferty, the teachings and example of Jesus made the answer clear: "Ye followers of the Prince of Peace, disarm yourselves," for "the weapons of our warfare are not carnal." Afterward, the *Evangel* took a sharply pacifist turn.

The wave of pacifist consensus crested in the summer of 1915 with a series of antiwar articles by Azusa Street veteran Frank Bartleman. Like a fierce Old Testament prophet, Bartleman fulminated against the sin and pride of all the warring nations and accused the United States of hypocrisy for war profiteering ("We had better pluck out the stars from our flag," he sneered, "and instate dollar marks in their place"). Bartleman lamented the exploitation of common people by their rulers and decried the folly and idolatry of rabid patriotism. Finally, he cited the staggering scale of the war's destruction as proof of dispensationalism's grim anthropology. "All beautiful theories about the rapid development of the human race...are now fallen," he averred. "They are using all progress and development in science, etc., to blow men into hell." In addition to running Bartleman's articles, the *Evangel* published a categorical declaration of its own: "The Pentecostal people...are uncompromisingly opposed to war," it claimed, "having much the same spirit as the early Quakers, who would rather be shot themselves than that they should shed the blood of their fellow men."

Over the next three years, that apparent consensus dissolved into equivocation. The last of Bartleman's articles had seemed to take sides, and readers criticized his perceived German bias. Letters demanding neutrality or outright support for the Allied cause increased. By the fall of 1915, moreover, AG ministers had begun to join the chaplain corps in significant numbers. The *Evangel* trumpeted those efforts, lending them its unqualified support. To be sure, the *Evangel* continued to publish articles by pacifists like British immigrant Stanley Frodsham and members of the British Booth-Clibborn family. But these were tactful, moderate voices; fire-breathing prophets like Bartleman dropped from its pages.

As U.S. involvement in the conflict approached, the *Evangel* balanced statements of pacifism with declarations of Pentecostal loyalty to the government. It prominently displayed New Testament passages on obedience to proper authority, like Romans 13, and gave instructions on how to respectfully apply for conscientious objector status. Finally, Bell emerged as a counterpoint to the strict pacifists in the AG. "God has some bright Pentecostal soldiers in both the British and German armies," he allowed. But it was extremely difficult to maintain one's Christian experience in the military. "Most who start in Christians," he sighed, "backslide." Therefore, he urged readers to avoid serving in the military "until compelled to do so, either by law or in defense of our mothers, wives and children." In Bell's mind, sin in the camp loomed larger than sin on the battlefield. And certain circumstances might indeed justify combatant service.

Within weeks of the U.S. declaration of war, the Executive Presbytery of the AG issued a general resolution aimed at securing the right of conscientious objection for its members. The resolution affirmed the body's loyalty but declared that it was bound by such divine commands as "Thou shalt not kill," "Resist no evil," and "Love your enemies." Pentecostals, claimed the resolution, had always rejected "the spilling of blood of any man, or of offering resistance to any aggression." The AG would "fulfill all the obligations of loyal citizenship," it concluded, but "we cannot conscientiously participate in war and armed resistance which involves the actual destruction of human life." When the *Evangel* announced the resolution, however, editorial comments made it clear that there was less to the resolution than met the eye. "It is not intended to hinder anyone from taking up arms who may feel free to do so," explained the editors, "but we hope to secure the privilege of exemption ... for all who are real conscientious objectors." The resolution had been composed with War Department criteria for military exemption in mind, therefore, and did not set a standard of behavior to be imposed on church members.

Over the following months, the principle of conscientious objection was more honored in the breach than in the observance. The first of Bartleman's articles, "Present Day Conditions," had been circulating in tract form. During the summer of 1918, with the Espionage and Sedition Acts hanging over their heads, *Evangel* editors asked readers to "destroy this tract." Though surely well meaning and fine for times of peace, they explained, it was "entirely too radical for war times." Shortly thereafter, Bell broke openly with the pacifist line. A soldier who kills an enemy in a lawful war, he opined, is not a murderer so long as he does so without hatred in his heart.[3]

What are we to make, then, of the Pentecostal response to the Great War? In some respects, Pentecostal vacillation only mirrored that of the nation, which moved from opposition to fitful neutrality to war fever. The Pentecostal peace witness, never absolute, simply buckled under the wave of 100 percent Americanism that swept the nation after 1916. This held particularly true among the nascent denominations, whose organizational tendencies themselves bespoke a concern for social engagement and practical efficacy, and whose leaders were perhaps already inclined to tilt the balance of outsiderhood and access, radicalism and relevance, in a more conservative direction. There especially, the consuming desire to win souls at any cost merged with aspirations for respectability to dictate policies that would preserve an open door for the Pentecostal message in society at large. As a result, most Pentecostal denominations opted for a middle way, as did the AG. They declared their official pacifism, but garnished those declarations with noisy shows of patriotism. Liberty of conscience became the de facto guide.

Looking back, we find that every major Pentecostal body declared its official pacifism at some point during the war, but the movement could never build a true consensus around prophetic nonresistance. Clearly, it leaned heavily in a pacifist direction—one does not pen pacifist resolutions for a nonpacifist body—but nonpacifists were always part of the mix, and the sheer diversity of the movement made it difficult to reach anything more than fleeting or rhetorical uniformity. In addition, Pentecostal pacifism sprang from multiple sources: New Testament admonitions; a sectarian desire to remain separate from the world; the prophetic counterpoise of dispensationalism. These were not incompatible, and each supported a kind of pacifism. But not pacifism of the same kind. As a result, even those who claimed pacifism did not necessarily agree on what that teaching meant. Many proved to be lovers of peace but not strict pacifists.

The saints had to work out the implications of their faith on this point at the very time they were locked in disputes over the nature of God and the meaning of sanctification. As it turned out, the peace issue simply did not command attention or grip loyalties as viscerally as did these others, and so it remained an issue of the second rank. On the positive side, this meant that it would not be a major impediment to unity. Pacifism was a prevailing mood but not a shibboleth. As such, the question of nonresistance, left to the conscience of the individual, receded slowly into the shadow of other controversies.

CONFRONTING MODERNISM

The gathering social and cultural trends of the early 20th century, catalyzed by the Great War, produced seismic changes in the years that followed. Whereas the revolutions before the war—cities of steel and glass, soaring bridges, electricity and rails and belching behemoths of factories—had produced a new industrial order, those that followed seemed to produce new people. Captivated by their own novelty, Americans spoke of the "new woman" or the "new Negro" and recognized their age of mass consumption, mass media, and mass entertainment as a thoroughly "new era." Nothing illustrated the novelty of the day more than the fashions adopted by the first generation of post-suffrage women. Flipping the pages of a women's magazine from the late Victorian era takes us into an alien world. Amelia Earhart could walk into a room today and scarcely raise an eyebrow except in admiration.

The various transformations clustered under the heading of modernism, but in truth reactions against currents of change—the Red Scare, nativism, a revived Klan, and a militant movement within evangelical Protestantism known as fundamentalism—were equally vital to the 1920s. The essence of the age lay somewhere in the clash between dry town and jazz-drenched speakeasy.

The term *modernism* encompassed the changing values and mores of the day along with its social adjustments and technological wonders. But in the realm of ideas, particularly those relevant to religion, it denoted the fruition of a century of challenges to traditional assumptions in science, philosophy, and religion. In the sciences, Darwinism presented natural selection, not creation by divine fiat, as the origin of the species, and scientific naturalism dismissed the supernatural out of hand. In the social sciences, historicism stressed the historical nature of all phenomena, undermining religious claims to unchanging or transcendent truth, while the new discipline of sociology hinted at the socially constructed nature of belief systems themselves. Meanwhile, the study of world religions relativized the truth claims of any particular tradition. For conservative Christians, however, the greatest threat of all rose from the historical-critical study of the Bible, which exposed the complexity and historicity of its constituent parts and of their selection and transmission over time. For many, the results of that discipline, also known as "higher criticism," made faith in the Bible as the literal Word of God difficult; faith in its inerrancy virtually impossible.

Religious reactions to modernism carved a divide that still shapes the landscape of American Protestantism. The majority of mainline Protestants, particularly in the North, sought to accommodate these developments, reconceiving the ancient verities in light of new discoveries and adapting them to the modern worldview. Known as Protestant modernists, they hoped to protect the essence of Christianity from the acids of modernism and to ensure its continuing relevance to the lives of thoughtful men and women.

Many followed the lead of German philosopher and theologian Friedrich Schleiermacher, who located the wellspring of religion in a transcendent realm of immediate apprehension beyond the reach of the scientific method. Schleiermacher had been deeply influenced by German pietism and recast its affective spirituality—a kind of spiritual empiricism wherein one's inner experience provided the surest evidence of the truth of divine things—into a philosophical defense against Enlightenment skepticism. The outcome was a truce that allowed science to explain the "phenomenal" realm (the material forms in which religion is clothed) while preserving the essence of religion in a "noumenal" realm apprehended through precognitive religious feeling.

Others, including those evangelicals most akin to Pentecostals in their theological views, drew a line in the sand. Taking their name from a series of short books published in the years just prior to the war, they came to be known as fundamentalists. The intellectual leadership of the movement came from Protestant rationalists like Princeton Theological Seminary greats Benjamin B. Warfield and J. Gresham Machen, who synthesized realist philosophy and systematic theology into an impressive defense of Christian Orthodoxy. Such men would tolerate no dichotomy between the noumenal and the phenomenal, and they staunchly defended the reality of absolute, divinely revealed truth grounded in an inerrant Bible.

Pentecostals, however, followed a third way, and their response to modernism distinguished them from the fundamentalist intelligentsia just as their travail over military service had distinguished them from evangelicals at large. In one sense, it is not surprising that Pentecostals should have followed their own path; a heavy stigma still hung about the movement, and most fundamentalists denounced perceived Pentecostal fanaticism as severely as they did modernist compromise. But the nature of the Pentecostal third way bears analysis.

Pentecostals held to the "fundamentals" as tenaciously as any fundamentalist. Yet, as scholars from Joseph E. Campbell to Grant Wacker have observed, they remained relatively unvexed by theological modernism. Moreover, the deeply affective and experiential character of Pentecostal spirituality contained striking parallels to that of Protestant modernism, though transposed into a plainfolk key. "We need no more theology or theory," exclaimed Frank Bartleman, perhaps with Presbyterian divines like Machen in mind. "Away with such foolish bondage! Follow your Heart! Believe in your own heart's hunger, and go ahead for God."[4] The priority of experience did not mean that correct belief was unimportant. But it did mean that—with some exceptions like the Oneness controversy—most Pentecostal disputes concerned belief *about* experience.

Pentecostal faith, that is, rested on the same pietistic epistemology that had underwritten Schleiermacher's response to Enlightenment skepticism. The immediate apprehension of divine things—a true "sense" of the soul touched by the Spirit—provided sure and sufficient evidence validating what the saints read in their Bibles. Holy Ghost experience is what turned the dead letter into Living Truth. Furthermore, Pentecostals seemed instinctively to understand that no modification of the original pietistic formula was needed, which spared them the intellectual contortions of modernists and fundamentalists alike. They had no quibble with the details of fundamentalist exposés of modernist "sleight of hand" or scholarly demonstrations of biblical inerrancy and the unscientific nature of evolution. But they were all perfectly unnecessary when a single earth-shaking encounter with the Holy Ghost could do that and more in a transforming instant.

The modifications, it seemed, were demanded only by the nature and social goals of mainstream Protestantism, whose leaders in both corners of the ring wished to engage elite secular culture on terms that culture would respect and perhaps find persuasive. Unlike modernists and scholarly fundamentalists, however, Pentecostals felt no compunction to frame their arguments in the categories of science and philosophy. They dwelt in plainfolk America, and plainfolk Americans had spent a couple of centuries discrediting intellectual and cultural elites; their approbation was generally avoided, not pursued. Experts and intellectuals might be called upon selectively to vouch for one or another point of dispute, but they were more often foils against which to demonstrate the greater wisdom of the common person. Since Pentecostals presupposed inner spiritual experience as the most valid path to certainty about religious truth, and since the distant world of the academy held little persuasive force either for them or for those they hoped to reach, nothing prevented Pentecostals from continuing to preach and practice a brand of Christianity as unabashedly literal as that of any 19th-century camp-meeting revivalist. Regardless of what was happening among the intellectual elite, the influence of historicism, scientific naturalism, and philosophical relativism had not so permeated popular culture as to seriously hinder the prosperity of a new edition of old-time religion, particularly one so keenly tuned to the sociological and technological dimensions of the modern age.

Pentecostalism, therefore, continued on its paradoxical third way, unscathed and relatively unperturbed by the corrosive winds of intellectual modernism. Soon, it would indeed gravitate toward those who shared its theological commitments and moral values, but for a brief while it held a middle ground, where its individualistic, experiential assumptions and progressive spirit resembled Protestant modernists while its doctrinal commitments, biblical literalism, and class affiliations echoed the grassroots—if not the institutional elites—of fundamentalism.

This paradoxical stance vis-à-vis modernity cut most acutely through the sphere of popular culture. The saints rejected new morality out of hand; there was no place for Edna St. Vincent Millay in Pentecostalism, and the typical minister blasted sin high and low, new and old, with the lusty gusto of a Billy Sunday. Yet the movement proved surprisingly adaptive to popular styles in many other areas, with the exception of women's fashions that were deemed immodest. Where mainline Protestants often joined modernist theology to traditional liturgy and church architecture, Pentecostals held the orthodox line but promiscuously imported popular music and instrumentation into their worship, and they conducted that worship in virtually any facility that made itself available, from abandoned taverns to old movie theaters.

No one better exemplified that distinctive fusion of tradition and modernity than did Aimee Semple McPherson, a Canadian-born evangelist who made her name under the bright lights of Los Angeles. Known at the height of her fame as "the world's most pulchritudinous evangelist," she would set the mold, by breaking the mold, for many Pentecostals to come.

Born Aimee Elizabeth Kennedy in Lower Ontario in 1890, she converted to Pentecostalism in 1907 and promptly married the evangelist whose message had prompted her conversion, Robert James Semple. In 1909 they moved to Chicago, where both were ordained by William H. Durham at his North Avenue Mission. The following year, Robert and a pregnant Aimee set out for the mission fields of China. Tragically, Robert succumbed to malaria shortly upon their arrival in Hong Kong. Aimee gave birth to their only child, Roberta Semple, and returned to the United States. Settling in New York City, the widowed mother met and married a divorced businessman, Harold McPherson, with whom she had a son, Rolf McPherson, in 1913.

In her first marriage, Aimee had been a partner in ministry. In her second, she was a mother of two facing traditional domestic expectations. For McPherson, the life of marital tranquility foundered on what Betty Freidan would later call "the problem that has no name." Comfortably situated in her middle-class home, she seemed to have all the makings of wifely bliss. "What right have you to fret and pine like this?" she asked herself. "Just look at that mahogany parlor furniture and the big brass beds.... Why aren't you glad to have a home like this for the babies, as any other mother would be?"[5] A later generation of women would answer that question by citing repressive social norms, the dissonance between putative feminine ideals and the unrealized potential of aspiring women. McPherson's answer was simpler and more direct. God had called her to preach; she was resisting the call, and suffering the consequences.

In 1915, McPherson swapped domesticity for the sawdust trail, to the detriment of her marriage—it ended in 1921—but the lasting benefit of her career and the Pentecostal movement. The savvy evangelist combined feminine charm and dramatic flair with clarity of message, and her cross-country tours soon packed spellbound throngs into the largest tents and venues. In 1917 she added a monthly magazine, *The Bridal Call*, to publicize her burgeoning ministry, and she later refashioned A. B. Simpson's fourfold gospel into her personal trademark, the Foursquare Gospel, which proclaimed Jesus as Savior, Baptizer with the Holy Spirit, Healer, and Soon-Coming King.

In 1918, McPherson made Los Angeles her base of operations. It was the perfect marriage of audience and performer. Her theatrical style and knack for sensation entranced Los Angeles, then emerging as the center of the nation's film industry, and she quickly emerged as one of the city's most famous residents. When McPherson's local following swelled into the thousands, she began to envision a domed facility capacious enough to accommodate it. Finally, in 1923, the imposing, 5,000-seat Angelus Temple—Pentecostalism's first megachurch—opened to overflow crowds. Situated in the fashionable Echo Park district, Angelus Temple drew an increasingly middle-class audience sprinkled with celebrity converts and public figures.

McPherson became the nation's first female radio personality in 1924 when she launched KFSG radio, only the fifth religious radio station in the United States. The enterprising Pentecostal embraced the new medium as "a beautiful priceless gift from the loving Hand of our Father God," and raised 250-foot radio towers on either side of the Temple's 110-foot dome—twin monuments to modernity flashing her Foursquare Gospel across the land. In social and cultural terms, this was about as far as one could get from Azusa Street, 1906.

By every account, McPherson was an extraordinary pulpit performer. Her Sunday services evolved into extravagant pageants complete with lavish sets, flashy costumes, and theatrical props that sometimes included live circus animals. Critics cheered her "matchless" timing and "uncanny" dramatic instincts. The riveting drama in McPherson's personal life, moreover, easily matched that on the Angelus Temple stage, as in the case of her mysterious 1926 disappearance amid rumors of an affair with her radio engineer, and her equally mysterious return from the alleged kidnapping ordeal five weeks later.

McPherson made her most enduring mark, however, not as a pulpit performer but as an institution builder. In 1923 she founded LIFE (Lighthouse for International Foursquare Evangelism) Bible College, which her increasing wealth and fame allowed her to staff with prominent scholars. Four years later, she capped her career by founding the International Church of the Foursquare Gospel. Within a decade of making Los Angeles her home, McPherson's ministry had blossomed into a full-fledged denomination.

Viewed from one perspective, McPherson was a singular figure, the exception rather than the rule among Pentecostals. Certainly, she and her followers were more culturally assimilated, more socially and politically engaged, and less bound to the moralistic heritage of Holiness than the average Pentecostal of their day. Yet McPherson perfectly incarnated what noted scholar Grant Wacker has called the "genius" of the movement: its ability to hold antinomies—pragmatism and primitivism, modernity and tradition, supernaturalism and entrepreneurialism—in "productive tension."[6] In the garish flare of her clashing contradictions, no one better encompassed the essence of Pentecostalism, indeed of America in the New Age, than did Aimee Semple McPherson.

PENTECOSTALISM BETWEEN THE WARS: GROWTH AND INSTITUTIONALIZATION

Throughout the 1920s and 1930s, American Pentecostalism enjoyed impressive numerical growth. Indeed, the national tragedy of the Great Depression seemed to enhance the young movement's appeal. Ironically, observers of mainstream religion had predicted such an effect, but as the 1930s progressed, they instead documented growing secularism and a relative malaise among the major religious institutions of the day. As a result, in U.S. religious history the 1930s was for a time construed as a period of stagnation. This construal, however, derived from a species of wish projection or selective perception that rendered mainstream observers blind to robust growth outside the margins of their sampling pool. Particularly after the public relations beating administered to fundamentalists and their religious kin at the Scopes Trial in Dayton, Tennessee, the mainstream media largely dismissed fundamentalists and "holy rollers," assigning to them the irrelevance they felt they so richly deserved.

The reality was far different. Despite public humiliation at the hands of critics like H. L. Mencken, the fundamentalists had prevailed at Dayton legally, and both they and their alienated Pentecostal kin flourished in the years that followed. Indeed, a triumphant A. J. Tomlinson could hardly contain his euphoria over the success that buoyed his branch of the movement in the 1930s. "I do not understand why people want to go back to the early Church," he complained. "I admit those were great days... but look what we are and what is just ahead." When Tomlinson peered out his window, he saw a different picture than did the Menckens of the world. "This is our time," he exulted. And the numbers backed him up. With the AG leading the way (its membership tripled, from 50,000 to 150,000, between 1926 and 1936) perhaps half a million Americans had cast their lot with the Pentecostals by the end of the 1930s.[7]

As membership grew, the institutional face of Pentecostalism expanded and ramified, bringing higher standards of professionalism and rising social aspirations to every branch of the movement. As often as not, schism turned the wheels of progress.

In 1923 a severe disruption broke the Church of God into two separate denominations. At the center of the controversy stood Tomlinson, the genial autocrat who had held sway over the body for the previous 20 years. On the surface, the dispute concerned Tomlinson's arbitrary use of church funds, but the underlying cause spoke to trends that would reorient governance throughout American Pentecostalism.

By the 1920s, a shift in the principles of management had taken hold in U.S. industry and government. The ideal of benevolent autocracy—the swashbuckling captain of industry of Gilded Age lore—lost appeal, and a new luster attached to governing committees, with their promise of regularity and expertise. In that climate, Pentecostal denominations saw a rise in two related phenomena: constitutionalism and rule by committee. Some degree of committee rule—as, for example, through general councils or boards of elders—had biblical warrant and was already well established, so increases here proved relatively uncontroversial. Constitutions, however, were an entirely different matter. Like statements of faith, they seemed to fly in the face of the movement's ecclesiological assumptions, which upheld the Bible as the only rule of faith and the Holy Spirit as the only guide. But the tide shifted.

Tomlinson had formed a council of elders in 1916, based on his understanding that such a council had advised Saint James in his administration of the see of Jerusalem. Five years later, that council secured the passage of a constitution, which limited Tomlinson's power and expanded its own. A showdown between Tomlinson and the elders ensued that culminated in 1923, when each side excommunicated the other. The majority of the denomination's members followed the elders, but a large minority remained loyal to the patriarch. After a protracted battle over control of the church name, the elders' faction came to be known as the Church of God (Cleveland, Tennessee), the Tomlinson faction as the Church of God of Prophecy. Despite the disruption, both bodies regrouped and grew steadily over the following years.

In neighboring precincts of Holiness Pentecostalism, a squabble over divine healing shook the Pentecostal Holiness Church. Moderates, who wished to supplement the power of faith with an occasional dose of orthodox medicine, left in 1921 to found the Congregational Holiness Church. The black United Holy Church of America suffered two successive blows. In 1924, Philadelphia pastor Ida Robinson defected to form the Mount Sinai Holy Church of America, thus securing full rights of ordination for women. Then, five years later, a group loyal to evangelist Brumfield Johnson organized as the Mount Calvary Holy Church of America.

Another addition to the Holiness Pentecostal ranks arrived, unexpectedly, from dissension within Finished Work efforts among Latinos in the West and Southwest. By the 1920s, a thriving Latino wing of the AG had emerged, largely through the agency of evangelist Carrie Judd Montgomery and missionaries like Alice Luce and Henry C. Ball. That development had been accompanied, however, by considerable tension over white paternalism, and a number of Latino congregations had begun to aspire to independence. Those sentiments catalyzed around charismatic Mexican evangelist Francisco Olazábal, "El Azteca," who broke with the AG to found the Latin American Council of Christian Churches in 1923. By the 1930s, Olazábal had taken a Holiness turn, and his rapidly growing organization might well have affiliated with the Church of God of Prophecy had it not been for his untimely death in an automobile accident in 1937.

Holiness Pentecostalism proved to be the rule, not the exception, as Pentecostals of every stripe practiced the ecclesial art of multiplying by dividing. No group suffered more fractures than did the Pentecostal Assemblies of the World (PAW). In 1919, a spat with other leaders prompted Robert Lawson to create the Church of Our Lord Jesus Christ of the Apostolic Faith. Lawson's church itself subdivided in 1930, when Sherrod C. Johnson set up a rival organization with an almost identical name, the Church of the Lord Jesus Christ of the Apostolic Faith.

From its inception, the PAW had struggled to maintain its interracial vision—an almost heroic goal in light of the resurgent racism of the day and in view of the fact that Indianapolis, the young denomination's headquarters, was home to the Ku Klux Klan throughout most of the 1920s. The PAW's interracial vision eventually weakened, though, and in 1924 the denomination split largely along race lines. Negotiations among the various groups continued, however, and the majority reunited in 1931 as the Pentecostal Assemblies of Jesus Christ.

That union proved fleeting. A contingent of African Americans, unhappy with the manner in which the new union had been effected and distressed by its abandonment of episcopal polity, revived the PAW. They were joined by most of the remaining African Americans when the Pentecostal Assemblies of Jesus Christ voted to hold its 1937 convention in Tulsa, Oklahoma, a racially segregated city that in 1921 had witnessed one of the worst race riots in U.S. history, with whites burning entire African American neighborhoods to the ground. Finally, in 1945, the majority of whites merged into the United Pentecostal Church, International, creating the nation's largest Oneness Pentecostal body.

While the bonds of fellowship between whites and African Americans unraveled, Oneness Latinos made their own escape. The Apostolic Assembly of Faith in Christ Jesus (Asamblea Apostólica de la Fe en Cristo Jesús, Inc.), had affiliated with the PAW in the prior decade's flush of Oneness unity. Amid the turmoil described above, it now severed those ties and followed its new presiding bishop, Antonio Castañeda Nava, on a course of independence and binational fellowship with sister congregations south of the border.

The organizational fertility of Finished Work Pentecostals equaled that of their Holiness and Oneness kin. As noted, the Statement of Fundamental Truths issued by the AG in 1916 effectively dislodged the Oneness faction from its midst. But the statement hit far more than its intended target, alienating many Trinitarians who recognized encroaching denominationalism when they saw it. Among them was John C. Sinclair, a Scots ex-Presbyterian caught between love of liberty and the manifest advantages of organization. Three years after his resignation from the AG, Sinclair and several colleagues, including George Brinkman, publisher of *The Pentecostal Herald*, tried to strike the balance that in their minds the AG had missed, founding an association now known as the Pentecostal Church of God.

Elsewhere, a rather intriguing symmetry brought offshoots of McPherson's Church of the Foursquare Gospel and Florence Crawford's Apostolic Faith—the two West Coast denominations founded by women—into union. In 1919 Fred Hornshuh, dismissed from the Apostolic Faith over a dispute with Crawford, established the Bible Standard Mission, later the Bible Standard Church. While Hornshuh's organization gained footing, discontent gathered among some of McPherson's flock over her flamboyant style, rumors of immorality surrounding her 1926 "kidnapping," and questions of ecclesiology. Her 1931 marriage to third husband David Hutton dropped the last straw, and several congregations followed John R. Richey into the Open Bible Evangelistic Association. Four years later, the two groups merged to form the Open Bible Standard Evangelistic Association, known after 1940 as the Open Bible Standard Church.[8]

The rise of Pentecostal organizations signaled a new era of intra-Pentecostal competition. Interchange certainly continued, as for example in the mass meetings of traveling evangelists like F. F. Bosworth, Charles S. Price, and Raymond T. Richey—figures who would lay the groundwork for a new generation of healing evangelists to come. That being said, as denominational walls went up, the pull of institutional loyalty and the push of remembered injuries redrew the pathways of Pentecost. Leaders urged members to show devotion to their own programs and publications, and denominational identity began to take hold.

Within any given denomination, that process worked in favor of greater uniformity or standardization. But it increased diversity within the movement as a whole, whose embrace now stretched from world-rejecting sects with strict codes of dress and comportment to West Coast bodies that blended rather easily into the currents of the day. Despite their differences, however, virtually all of the denominations gravitated toward increased professionalism, more centralized authority, and higher expectations for regularity and achievement. By the end of the 1920s, for example, all of the leading bodies had established Bible colleges or training institutes.

In these and other ways, the arc of progress bent the movement slowly toward the mainstream. Proximity to the mainstream, however, increased stress at those points where the movement remained out of step with mainstream norms. These included residual pacifism, certainly, but also the matters of race and gender. Frank Bartleman had famously boasted that at Azusa Street, "the 'color line' was washed away in the blood."[9] As we have seen, it came back. By the end of the 1930s, virtually all Pentecostal denominations had segregated along racial lines, either in toto or by separating the races into different wings of a single body.

Yet minorities continued to be overrepresented in the movement, and both the ideal of interracial worship and even its actual practice persisted, though in a much diminished state. The Tomlinson branch of the Church of God, for example, preached a "speckled bird" theology according to which Jeremiah 12:9 ("Mine heritage is unto me as a speckled bird") required the church to be interracial, and Tomlinson made laudable efforts to realize that ideal despite his location in the Jim Crow South. The segregation of Pentecostalism in the 1920s and 1930s is certainly disappointing in light of the movement's origins. Yet viewed in the context of its times and in relation to its peers, Pentecostalism still placed in the vanguard of race relations in pre–World War II America.

Ambivalence toward women in ministry also increased as the movement edged toward the mainstream. To be sure, a degree of ambiguity had always surrounded the matter. Virtually all Pentecostals had affirmed the prophetic role of women whereby they proclaimed the Word under the anointing of the Holy Spirit, but when it came to the priestly role of ordained ministry, the consensus had ended, with many distinguishing between male and female prerogatives in ways that cut more or less along this prophetic/priestly line. That distinction gathered strength as the movement acculturated.

Nevertheless, when men sought to restrict women's roles, women fought back. "If Mary the mother of Jesus could carry the Word of God in her womb," fumed Ida Robinson, "why can't holy women carry the word of God in their mouth?" Likewise, Mable Smith rebutted efforts to limit women in the Church of God in Christ. "After God has removed the yokes from our necks men have tried to put them back on us," she opined. "Which is better," Smith asked the "mothers" of her church, "to be appointed by a man to do a work or to be anointed by God to do it?"[10] In many cases, women actually regained lost ground, as when a 1933 resolution barring women from pastoral ministry in the AG was overturned two years later. Despite setbacks, then, Pentecostal women kept a step ahead of their mainstream peers.

WAR AND RAPPROCHEMENT

By the mid-1930s, tremors of an impending second Great War had disturbed Europe's fragile peace. There, a militantly nationalist ideology, fascism, had taken hold, while in Asia, Japan aggressively expanded its Greater East Asia Co-Prosperity Sphere. When Germany invaded Poland in the autumn of 1939, Europe again erupted in open conflict. The U.S. war machine rumbled to life, ending the economic hardship of the Great Depression but introducing the specter of U.S. involvement in yet another global struggle. Two years later, with the Japanese attack on Pearl Harbor, the United States was once again a nation at war.

For pacifists, the moral dilemma struck home a full year before Pearl Harbor, when the Selective Service and Training Act of 1940 required men between the ages of 21 and 35 to register for the nation's first peacetime draft. The Pentecostal movement facing that dilemma, however, had greatly changed since 1918. Pacifism still existed, but in much-attenuated form. Ernest S. Williams, general superintendent of the AG, restated the denomination's official position and recommended noncombatant service to his draft-age men. But his advice went largely unheeded as tens of thousands of young Pentecostal men from every branch of the movement marched off to serve their country on the battlefields of Europe and Asia.

The capitulation was not complete: most denominations continued to echo their pacifist heritage by at least recommending noncombatant service, even if they did not require it, and a smattering of Pentecostals did file as conscientious objectors. But some denominations broke ranks. The currents of change were unmistakable, and when it came to change, Aimee Semple McPherson, as usual, led the way.

When debate over military service reignited in the 1930s, pacifists in the International Church of the Foursquare Gospel sought to impose conscientious objection on all of its ministers. McPherson intervened, engineering an ambiguous policy that endorsed conscientious objection but allowed members to act as their consciences dictated. Once the United States entered the war, however, the ambiguity ceased. McPherson cheered the national cause and persuaded her church to repeal its endorsement of conscientious objection. She became one of the leading war fundraisers in Southern California, and won praise from the Office of War Information for using KFSG to boost the war effort. The low point of her pro-war jingoism came in 1943, when she lobbied against the prospect of releasing Japanese Americans from their internment camps.

By the end of the war, the mission of Christianity and the mission of the United States had merged in her mind. "I am for America and America is for Jesus Christ," she proclaimed. "The flag of America and the church.... stand or fall together!"[11] For McPherson, rejection of pacifism and fervent support for the national war effort were flip sides of the same coin. It was the coin of civil religion, and it marked the end of apoliticism for those who held it.

Few Pentecostals went so far as McPherson, but her actions testify to the power of the Second World War as a syncretizing event. It unleashed socially centripetal forces that drew diverse Americans to a commonly phrased if differently perceived center marked out by potent terms such as Americanism and democracy. The war, in short, formed the condition for the possibility of the much-vaunted era of consensus to follow.

For Pentecostals, the war interacted with preexisting trends to inaugurate a period of cultural rapprochement. Two generations of growth and institutionalization had opened many of the movement's largest bodies to the wartime impulse toward social solidarity and religious association. As a result, they drew nearer to their fellow evangelicals, even as their fellow evangelicals drew nearer to the American mainstream. And Pentecostals drew nearer to one another as well, as parts of their fractured universe slowly recovered a lost sense of Pentecostal accord.

In 1942, a group of comparatively broad-minded evangelical leaders formed the National Association of Evangelicals (NAE) as a counterpoise to the more liberal Federal Council of Churches. Some of the chief organizers, being familiar with Pentecostalism, made overtures to its leading denominations. This move spoke volumes not only about the changes occurring within Pentecostalism, but about those reshaping fundamentalism as well: as recently as 1928, the World's Christian Fundamentals Association had denounced the "present wave of Modern Pentecostalism," as "a menace" and "a real injury to sane testimony of Fundamental Christians."

By the 1940s, however, a new generation of fundamentalist leaders hoped to shake the movement's reputation for dour antimodernism and narrow intolerance. Men like James Elwin Wright, Harold John Ockenga, and Will Houghton preferred to be called evangelicals, and they combined a vigorous intellectual defense of Christian orthodoxy with an engaged, irenic, forward-looking posture. In that spirit, they invited Pentecostal groups to join their new association, and the AG, the Church of God (Cleveland, Tennessee), the Pentecostal Holiness Church, and the Open Bible Standard Church accepted, becoming charter members of the NAE. Others soon followed, and Pentecostalism took its first major step toward alliance with the broader evangelical world.

Voices for intra-Pentecostal ecumenicity had risen in the wilderness for decades, and in the 1930s AG leaders had attempted to organize a world conference of Pentecostals. The war intervened, but afterward, aided by rising ecumenical star David J. du Plessis, that dream materialized when the World Pentecostal Conference (known after 1958 as the Pentecostal World Conference) convened in Zurich, Switzerland, in 1947. Back in the United States, the birth of the NAE facilitated similar efforts among Pentecostals. Its four Pentecostal charter members joined with the International Church of the Foursquare Gospel in 1948 to form the Pentecostal Fellowship of North America, which brought white Holiness and Finished Work Pentecostals into constructive dialogue. The absence of African Americans, however, and the explicit exclusion of Oneness Pentecostals highlighted the daunting obstacles to full unity that still remained.

Pentecostalism, nevertheless, was opening up to the world around it. Decades of growth and change had prepared it now to reach out, transforming others in the very process of itself being transformed.

But the new opportunities open to the movement came at a price. Growing nationalism and increasing ease in midcentury America suggested that many Pentecostals had embraced the unresolved contradiction endemic to American dispensationalism, according to which "America was simultaneously Babylon and God's chosen nation."[12] For Pentecostals at midcentury, the weight had begun to shift toward the latter of those assumptions. In many respects, Pentecostalism had always been the quintessentially American religion. Now, it seemed ready to make America its home.

NOTES

1. A. J. Tomlinson, *Answering the Call of God* (Cleveland, TN: White Wing Publishing House, ca. 1913), 9–10.

2. Jay Beaman, *Pentecostal Pacifism: The Origin, Development, and Rejection of Pacific Belief among the Pentecostals* (Hillsboro, KS: Center for Mennonite Studies, 1989); "Coming struggle" is Charles Parham, *The Everlasting Gospel* (Baxter Springs, KS: Apostolic Faith Bible College, 1911), 28; "end of this age" is quoted in Sarah Parham, *The Life of Charles Parham* (Joplin, MO: Tri-State Printing, 1930), 274.

3. This reconstruction is based on Roger Robins, "A Chronology of Peace: Attitudes toward War and Peace in the Assemblies of God," *Pneuma: The Journal for the Society of Pentecostal Studies*, Spring 1984, 3–25. For a more comprehensive treatment, see Paul Alexander, *Peace to War: Shifting Allegiances in the Assemblies of God* (Telford, PA: Cascadia Publishing House, 2009).

4. Frank Bartleman, *How Pentecost Came to Los Angeles* (Los Angeles: Frank Bartleman, 1925), 91.

5. Matthew Sutton, *Aimee Semple McPherson and the Resurrection of Christian America* (Cambridge, MA: Harvard University Press, 2007), 12.

6. Grant Wacker, *Heaven Below: Early Pentecostals and American Culture* (Cambridge, MA: Harvard University Press, 2001), 10. For more on McPherson, see Sutton, cited above, and Edith Blumhofer, *Aimee Semple McPherson: Everybody's Sister* (Grand Rapids, MI: Wm. B. Eerdmans Publishing, 1993).

7. Tomlinson is quoted in Lillie Duggar, *A. J. Tomlinson* (Cleveland, TN: White Wing Publishing House, 1964), 389. Adherence estimates are based on U.S. Census Bureau data and Sydney Ahlstrom, *A Religious History of the American People* (New Haven, CT: Yale University Press, 1973), 920.

8. For denominational histories, see relevant entries in Stanley Burgess and Eduard Van Der Maas, eds., *The New International Dictionary of Pentecostal and Charismatic Movements*, rev. ed. (Grand Rapids, MI: Zondervan, 2003).

9. Bartleman, 54.

10. Quotes are from Felton Best, "Loosing the Women: African-American Women and Leadership in the Pentecostal Church, 1890–Present," paper presented to the 24th Meeting of the Society for Pentecostal Studies, November 10–12, 1994, Wheaton, Illinois.

11. Based on Sutton, 254–266.

12. George Marsden, with reference to Fundamentalists, in *Fundamentalism and American Culture*, 2nd ed. (New York: Oxford University Press, 2006), 247.

CHAPTER 4

America's Pentecost

In the generation that followed World War II, American Pentecostalism came fully of age. Its long trajectory of growth and evolution continued, now accelerated by the paradoxically reciprocal effects of two very different influences. While savvy cadres of executives and bureaucrats guided the movement's leading denominations to new heights of effectiveness, a wave of mesmerizing healing evangelists seized the popular imagination, broadcasting the Pentecostal ethos further than it had ever gone before. Often rivals, sometimes adversaries, together they transformed Pentecostalism into a recognized force in U.S. religion. Indeed, more than a force, it became a major agent of cultural change, inspiring a revolution in spiritual manners and mores that rippled across American Christianity, Protestant and Catholic alike. By the mid-1970s, the upper echelons of Pentecostalism had earned a measure of social respectability—in the United States as nowhere else, the standard wage paid to success—and had tasted the first fruits of temporal power to a degree that early Pentecostals would hardly have imagined, or perhaps even have desired.

GOOD NEWS FOR MODERN MAN

Most scholars and cultural critics of the time considered Pentecostalism to be decidedly antimodern. Yet its message, social instincts, and organizational structures proved well suited to the modern realities of the postwar United States. The bombs that fell on Hiroshima and Nagasaki had marked the end of a war and the beginning of an era, with a cosmic struggle against communism superseding the battle against Axis titans as a spur to solidarity and nationalism. Thereafter, Cold War confrontations and proxy wars kept Americans in the grip of uncertainty, feeling their way through a world of stark antinomies: the greatest period of sustained economic growth that the middle class had ever seen, yet haunted by the anxious specters of nuclear attack from afar and moral and political subversion at home. Nothing more fully embodied this mingling of fear and prosperity than the many suburban dream homes that came equipped with their own bomb shelters.

Pentecostals of every brand had a ready answer for these troubled times—a message of deliverance, certitude, and ultimate victory. In many respects, Cold War realities rendered the Pentecostal gospel more plausible. The perceived threat of sudden, imminent destruction, which tossed grade school children beneath their desks in simulated defense against a Soviet nuclear attack, fostered a doomsday mood that opened minds to apocalyptic scenarios of a more traditional kind, like that outlined in dispensationalism. And for those stressed by the conformist pressures of loyalty crusades and the corporate hegemony of "organization men," Pentecostalism offered the subcultural pleasures of intense experience and frank supernaturalism in an ecclesial package that still affirmed the core values of Americanism.

The so-called era of consensus, of course, was anything but. This was the America of rock 'n' roll, the Beatniks, civil rights, and the Kinsey Report, where rising immorality, juvenile delinquency, and social disorder ranked just behind communism in conservative fears of the day. During the 1960s, moreover, those seeds of nonconformity and discontent blossomed into widespread social unrest and a provocative counterculture, which seemed to place the very fabric of society at risk. Here also, Pentecostalism addressed the perceived needs of the day, offering a bulwark against cultural erosion while subtly incorporating elements of new fads in an effort to reach youth enthralled by them.

Pentecostalism also responded effectively to the postwar edition of America's trademark demographic mobility. That mobility was twofold. First, a complex pattern of regional migration sent large numbers of African Americans into the industrial centers of the Northeast and Great Lakes—a continuation of prewar patterns—while whites left those same regions for the Sun Belt South. Meanwhile, strong currents carried Americans of all races and regions to the West Coast. Pentecostals rode all of these waves and seized the opportunities that came to them, whether as hosts or new arrivals. By the 1950s, the South had emerged as the heartland of American Pentecostalism, and Southern Pentecostal out-migration leavened and refreshed Pentecostal congregations throughout the country. At the same time, Sun Belt inmigration presented a new equation. Pentecostals had always gone to the people; now, the people were coming to them.

The second aspect of postwar mobility occurred within regions, as the latest and greatest wave of suburbanization transformed patterns of residence in every major urban center. With returning veterans helping to engineer first a marriage boom and then a baby boom, Americans flooded into newly constructed suburbs, which seemed to offer the American dream in a compact, affordable package. Suburbanization, in turn, was predicated on the nation's commitment to that icon of individualism, the automobile, as its primary means of transportation. Underwritten by the Interstate Highway Act of 1956, that commitment reconfigured how and where Americans lived, worked, and played around the presupposition of the automobile.

Demographic mobility in both of these forms produced an enormous demand for elective community, and postwar Pentecostals met that demand as adeptly as had their parents. Suburban Pentecostal churches sprang up across the landscape, and by the 1970s Pentecostal megachurches dotted the highways and bypasses of the nation's interstate system, offering convenient access, ample parking, communal warmth, and lively renditions of old-time religion, now modulated to a higher-toned key for upwardly mobile suburbanites.

PENTECOSTAL DENOMINATIONS:
BRICK, MORTAR, AND EVANGECOSTALISM

As the leading Pentecostal denominations met the challenges and took the opportunities of their day, they underwent two related developments. First, like Catholics and mainstream Protestants, they entered a brick and mortar phase, wherein institutional growth, bureaucratic expansion, and rising professionalism took the material form of new and larger facilities. Second, a new generation of gifted administrators helped bear them into the bosom of evangelicalism.

Brick and mortar Pentecostalism had both congregational and institutional manifestations. At the local level, Pentecostal congregations exchanged temporary or outgrown accommodations, including many unconventional sites of opportunity (theaters, store fronts, tents, and the like) for permanent structures in the churchly style. Among these were a number of lavish sanctuaries. At the institutional level, various denominations met expanding needs and symbolized their rising status with enlarged administrative buildings—as, for example, when the Pentecostal Church of God, in 1957, erected a four-story office building and a publishing house for its new headquarters in Joplin, Missouri. Larger bodies like the Church of God (Cleveland, Tennessee) and the Assemblies of God (AG) raised yet more impressive edifices.

Facilities of this kind bore visible witness to a trend toward bureaucratic formalism—the "transference of charisma from the man to the office," as Daniel Ramirez has noted of the Apostolic Assembly of Faith in Christ Jesus during this period.[1] Denominations in every branch of the movement enjoyed robust growth over the postwar years, and they responded by creating scores of programs and ministries to serve existing members or recruit new ones. These included publishing and educational endeavors in addition to targeted or cross-cultural ministries like service centers for military personnel, Jewish and Muslim outreach programs, student and youth evangelism departments, drug rehabilitation programs, orphanages, and homes for troubled teens and abused women.

As new programs were added or old ones subdivided, bureaucracy expanded, which produced new administrative challenges. Consequently, officials sought better ways to consolidate and extend their gains, coordinate their efforts, manage their resources, and supervise their burgeoning operations. The norms of professional management took hold, creating a climate in which skilled administrators like Thomas Zimmerman of the AG and R. Dennis Heard of the Pentecostal Church of God rose quickly through the ranks. Though validated by later results, this transition from a family to a corporate model of operation produced many casualties and was as painful to some as it was necessary in the eyes of its proponents.

Missions programs, beefed up and professionalized, ranked among the leading beneficiaries of these changes. And if denominational growth flagged, officials now did more than pray for a deeper anointing. They appointed committees to conduct institutional reviews and issue formal recommendations. The norms of professional management, moreover, carried political as well as administrative implications, nudging groups toward ideals of shared governance, representative polity, and regular mechanisms for the transfer of power such as term limits for elected officers.

Institutionalization of this kind joined with the upward mobility of adherents to raise the premium on higher education. Bible institutes added arts and sciences curriculum, and in 1955 the AG opened the first Pentecostal liberal arts institution, Evangel College, which sought and won regional accreditation a decade later. Meanwhile, as Bible institutes became Bible colleges, many sought accreditation from the Accrediting Association of Bible Colleges: the kind of formal imprimatur from outsiders that a previous generation would surely have scorned. With the opening of Oral Roberts University in 1965, Pentecostalism had its first full-scale university. A decade later, the AG and the Church of God (Cleveland, Tennessee) each added graduate schools for the advanced theological training of ministers and teachers.

Not all Pentecostals shared the thirst for formal learning; less-assimilated groups remained hostile at worst, wary at best, of these efforts to "be like all the nations." Among the leading denominations, however, interest soared. In the AG, for example, the percentage of members holding a college diploma tripled between 1960 and 1970, and a widening stream of third- and fourth-generation Pentecostals began to earn advanced degrees at prestigious institutions.[2]

Concomitant with these trends, an increasing number of professionals and persons of means surfaced among the faithful, which in turn fostered greater circumspection in worship at upscale congregations. When a woman interrupted one distinguished pastor's sermon by singing in the Spirit, he asked her to stop. She protested that the Spirit had bade her to sing, but the pastor countered that the Spirit had bade *him* to preach, and could hardly be thought to contradict himself.[3] The winds of the Spirit would henceforth blow through more regular channels.

Particularly in these socially aspiring circles, acculturation also loosened long-standing taboos concerning dress and popular entertainment, so that cosmetics, jewelry, sports activities, casual pastimes, and television watching began to filter into the subculture. Oneness Pentecostals like the United Pentecostal Church and Holiness bodies like the Church of God of Prophecy tried to hold the line, adhering to strict holiness mores and carrying forward the tradition of unrestrained Holy Ghost worship. But the majority was marching past Zion into the mainstream.

As Pentecostalism evolved, the world took notice. Prior to the 1950s, Pentecostalism functioned in the public mind largely as a form of exoticism, conjuring images of holy rollers and snake handlers. In 1945, for example, the *New York Times* had carried a feature on the Dolly Pond Church of God with Signs Following—a small serpent-handling group near Chattanooga, Tennessee—and deaths by snake bite made headlines throughout the 1940s.

In the 1950s, however, the national media began to change its tone. The new appraisal rose initially from ecumenical circles, where David du Plessis had followed up his World Pentecostal Conference success by opening dialogue with leaders of the World Council of Churches, many of whom had encountered vibrant Pentecostal movements overseas. Du Plessis pitched Pentecostalism as a third stream of Christianity, running parallel to historic Protestantism and Roman Catholicism, and that framework took hold. In the 1950s, Lesslie Newbigin and Henry Van Dusen each penned widely read accounts of the movement that credited it in precisely these terms, and in 1962, *Time* recognized Pentecostalism as the "fastest growing religious movement in the hemisphere."[4]

Pentecostalism, we have seen, took its first steps toward rapprochement with the wider evangelical world in the 1940s, when several predominantly white, Trinitarian bodies joined the National Association of Evangelicals (NAE). Now, amid these favorable trends, those denominations moved toward full evangelicalization. Pentecostal leaders built close alliances with evangelical counterparts, pursuing common interests in lobbying organizations like the National Religious Broadcasters and in parachurch agencies like Campus Crusade for Christ, founded by the Presbyterian evangelical Bill Bright in 1951. By the 1960s, most white, denominational Trinitarians were "firmly committed to the evangelical consensus," including "anticommunism, anti-Catholicism, and antiecumenism."[5] Pentecostals had warmed to evangelicals, and the feeling seemed mutual: In 1960, Thomas Zimmerman, general superintendent of the AG, was elected president of the NAE.

Evangelical identity had implications for broader Pentecostal relations. Although fundamentalists and modernists each tilted toward the middle in the postwar years (the latter taking a neo-orthodox turn while the former evolved into neo-evangelicals) those changes did little to bridge the chasm separating religious Americans. Becoming evangelical still meant openly aligning against the agents of mainline modernism, such as the worldwide ecumenical movement. Leaders of the World Council of Churches, as noted above, had extended an olive branch to Pentecostals, offering words of praise and cultivating ties with those few Pentecostals, like du Plessis, who would abide their company. Those overtures were not reciprocated. "Regardless of efforts of the World Council of Churches and the National Council of Churches who assay to call us 'brethren,'" Zimmerman grumbled to the 1961 Pentecostal World Conference, "we are miles apart."[6] In 1963, the AG officially condemned the ecumenical movement and forbade its ministers to cooperate with it at any level. Du Plessis was one of the first casualties. He surrendered his credentials and found himself ostracized from the inner circles of the Pentecostal World Conference, which he had helped to create.

Despite Pentecostalism's new evangelical identity, tensions lingered with more traditional evangelicals on the one hand, and their old Holiness kin on the other. Both still held Pentecostals at arm's length, willing to rub shoulders under the big tent of the NAE but careful to erect firewalls against glossolalia in their own denominations. Those residual tensions, however, did little to hinder Pentecostalism's emergence as a central pillar in a 20th-century Evangelical United Front.

REVITALIZING CHARISMA

The progress of leading Pentecostal denominations toward bureaucratic order and evangelical respectability did not go uncontested. Rather, it provoked revitalization movements among Pentecostals disdainful of gentrification and nostalgic for the free-flowing spirit and stark ecstasies of the remembered past. These saints felt that the 1940s had ushered in a period of declension, a falling away from the movement's original power and promise, indeed, from its "first love." The passing of first-generation giants like McPherson, Price, and Wigglesworth only compounded that sense of decline. Meanwhile, a new wave of millenarian expectation gathered under the shadow of the bomb, and perhaps more importantly, at the manger of the state of Israel, whose birth virtually all Pentecostals read as a precursor of the Second Coming. The time was ripe for revival.

From Canada and the upper Midwest, a New Order of the Latter Rain swept the dry plains of Pentecostalism. Meanwhile, a powerful deliverance movement erupted, led by iconic miracle workers who vied with one another for pride of place in the magnitude of their meetings and the scale of their stupefying wonders. Both of these lent fresh momentum to independent Pentecostalism, which, having resisted the lure of denominationalism, now swelled with infusions from an intra-Pentecostal wave of come-outers.

THE NEW ORDER OF THE LATTER RAIN

In 1948, a powerful outpouring of Pentecostal manifestations fell at Sharon Children's Homes and Schools in North Battleford, Saskatchewan, a ministry founded the previous fall by George and Ern Hawtin, Percy Hunt, and Herrick Holt. The first three had just broken with the Pentecostal Assemblies of Canada, while Holt held papers with the International Church of the Foursquare Gospel. Students and faculty at North Battleford reported many of the charismata of Azusa Street lore, such as "the heavenly choir," and felt sure they had recovered the spirit of that storied revival.

But the Sharon outpouring had its distinctive marks as well. These included the ascetic discipline of extended fasting (gleaned from evangelist Franklin Hall's *Atomic Power with God through Fasting and Prayer* [1946]); an emphasis on spiritual warfare and exorcism; the imparting of specific spiritual gifts through the laying on of hands; and the proclamation of a theocratic chain of command mediated through the fivefold ministry of apostles, prophets, evangelists, pastors, and teachers. In addition, Sharon's leaders curtly rejected denominationalism in favor of "full congregational sovereignty." No divinely called leader, they believed, should ever be pressed under the thumb of a bureaucrat.

Like early Pentecostals, the saints at Sharon viewed their own revival as the "latter rain" prophesied in Joel 2:28, which, in the dispensationalist scheme of things, marked the immediate prelude to the Rapture. Soon known as the New Order of the Latter Rain, the intensely millenarian movement spread rapidly. Camp meetings and conferences, promoted in *The Sharon Star*, drew visitors to North Battleford from across North America, while Sharon emissaries carried the tidings far and near.

The movement sparked controversy from its very inception. Latter Rain zealots denounced Pentecostal denominations, and virtually all of the denominations responded in kind, seeking to quench the new spirit with its perceived errors and excesses. Above all, critics warned of the incipient danger in New Order teachings about submission to apostolic authority, which seemed merely to exchange authoritarianism far away for authoritarianism near at home.

Despite the best efforts of its many detractors, New Order teaching made deep inroads among independent and denominational Pentecostals alike. Myrtle Beall's Bethesda Missionary Temple in Detroit and the Elim Bible Ministerial Assembly (later Elim Fellowship) of Lima, New York, emerged as New Order centers in the Great Lakes region, while out West, Thomas Wyatt's Wings of Healing Temple in Portland carried the flame. All major denominations suffered losses to the movement, the most prominent being *Pentecostal Evangel* editor Stanley Frodsham, but Scandinavian American Pentecostals were especially hard hit. Indeed, their largest body, the Independent Assemblies of God (now the Fellowship of Christian Assemblies), split when Latter Rain sympathizers left in 1951 to found the Independent Assemblies of God, International.[7]

DELIVERANCE!

The New Order of the Latter Rain left a deep imprint on postwar Pentecostalism, but it paled against a surge of healing evangelism that swept the movement, packing thousands into the capacious tents of scores of evangelists across the country and around the world. As the sheer magnitude of the phenomenon suggests, it sprang from a rare coincidence of social mood and a uniquely gifted generation of practitioners. The evangelists described their work as deliverance: deliverance from sin, sickness, and Satan. But it could be equally understood as a riveting blend of old-fashioned revivalism, faith healing, and prosperity teaching built on the laws of faith ("ask and ye shall receive") and the laws of divine reciprocity ("give and it will be given unto you").[8] The postwar healers did not invent their own tradition; they walked in the venerable steps of forerunners like F. F. Bosworth, Maria Woodworth-Etter, and Carrie Judd Montgomery, and their core doctrines had long pervaded Pentecostalism, high and low.[9] But what they accomplished exceeded anything that had come before.

There were almost as many styles of healing evangelism as there were evangelists, who ranged from the suave professionals to the two-fisted brawlers. Like the comic book superheroes of the day, each seemed to possess some signal trait, some distinguishing mark to set him or her apart from the field. The world of deliverance was intensely competitive, pushing some to extreme claims or practices in search of an angle or advantage. One evangelist declared that a sermon he had just preached had been supernaturally broadcast across the nation on television. Others boasted of holding the secret to immortality. Almost all practiced exorcism, but some made it a specialty, casting out "demons of sickness, of lies, of fornication, Hitler demons and divorce demons." Yet another proclaimed a breakthrough "bodyfelt salvation." It was "700% greater than ordinary healing power" and produced a Jesus fragrance that eliminated body odor and even killed bugs, making the saint "a Holy Ghost exterminator."[10] Notwithstanding differences of style, however, deliverance evangelists shared common traits and, above all, a common millenarian aspect, holding their audiences poised at the taut brink of that ultimate miracle, the Second Coming of Jesus Christ.

Many evangelists were spellbinding orators or gifted singers, but the centerpiece and drawing card of every meeting remained the direct encounter with the Holy, the moment when a gifted wonder worker stepped forward to practice the craft. At that sharp precipice, the fraught atmosphere of the tent, the urgent needs of the crowd, and the fervor of the evangelist combined to produce startling miracle events. The sick were healed, demons cast out, supernatural halos flared around anointed heads, and at times the dead were raised. Afterward, the accoutrements of affliction—crutches, wheelchairs, stretchers, braces, and bandages—would litter the perimeter of the tent, bearing silent witness to, in a word, *deliverance.*

Most healing evangelists began their careers in one or another Pentecostal denomination, but the more successful among them housed their ministries in independent corporations, published their own magazines, and raised enough funds to be self-sufficient. In the end, most shook their denominational chains, the better to seize opportunities as they found them. Yet, despite frequent tensions between deliverance evangelists and denominational officials, the two enjoyed reciprocal benefits, as denominational congregations and clergy helped to fill evangelists' tents and then shared the fruits of the publicity and personal conversions that emanated from them.

Viewed from the perspective of Pentecostal history, deliverance evangelism made two key contributions to the larger movement. First, because wonder workers lived and died by the mass meeting, they practiced a kind of tent-meeting ecumenism, deemphasizing controversial doctrines like sanctification and the Godhead in order to draw from the broadest possible spectrum. Deliverance evangelists were the only figures to span all branches of the Pentecostal movement, building grassroots alliances that exceeded the reach of organizations like the Pentecostal Fellowship of North America and the Pentecostal World Conference.

Second, the open borders of the tent gave access to seekers and sightseers of all religious backgrounds, making deliverance evangelism the principle port of transit for the Pentecostal message and mindset to the non-Pentecostal world. In these and other respects, William Branham, A. A. Allen, and Oral Roberts stand as exemplars of deliverance evangelism.

WILLIAM BRANHAM

William Marrion Branham was born to abject poverty not far from Louisville, Kentucky, and reared in the nearby southern Indiana town of Jeffersonville. Converted in his 20s, he rose to notoriety among local Baptists and in the 1930s founded Branham Tabernacle in Jeffersonville. Following the loss of his wife and child to illness in 1937, he began to conduct healing revivals in Oneness Pentecostal circles.

According to Branham, the turning point of his ministry came in 1946, when a visiting angel bestowed two gifts on him: the gift of healing and the gift of discerning the secrets of the heart. Afterward, the angel of the Lord would come to his side in his meetings and miraculously reveal explicit details about specific individuals, including their innermost sins and secrets. Furthermore, Branham's gift of healing included the ability to detect demons and diseases through vibrations in his left hand. With these gifts now at his disposal, Branham's ministry mushroomed into a national sensation. The soft-spoken seer regaled rapt audiences with accounts of his conversations with God and angels, but the truly electrifying moment always came when, angel at his side, he applied his prodigious gifts.

If 1946 marked the turning point for Branham's spiritual empowerment, 1947 marked the turning point for his evangelistic career, indeed, for the deliverance movement as a whole. Hoping to expand his ministry beyond Oneness circles in advance of a crusade in Vancouver, British Columbia, Branham recruited a man of impeccable Pentecostal credentials, James Gordon Lindsay, to serve as his publicist and campaign manager. Lindsay was a Parham convert, former John G. Lake associate, and pastor in good standing with the AG. His family traced its roots back through Finis Yoakum's Pisgah Home and Gardens all the way to Dowie's Holiness utopia at Zion, Illinois. Lindsay had ties throughout Trinitarian Pentecostalism, and his hiring proved to be a stroke of genius. The magazine Lindsay launched in 1948 to publicize Branham's meetings, *Voice of Healing*, evolved into a clearinghouse for the entire deliverance movement, with the ministry of Lindsay himself as the nearest thing it had to an organizational center. In addition to Lindsay, Branham coaxed Bosworth out of retirement and added Ern Baxter of North Battleford to his evangelistic team. The doors of Trinitarian Pentecostalism swung wide.

For the next decade, Branham packed tents, auditoriums, and stadiums across the nation with crowds matched only by those of his friendly rival, Oral Roberts. Tales of wonder accumulated, with the sick being healed and the possessed delivered at a mere word from the magnetic evangelist. In Los Angeles, William D. Upshaw, former congressman, cast aside his crutches of 60 years; in Jonesboro, Arkansas, a dead woman returned to life; in Houston, a news photographer captured a luminescent halo hovering just above the evangelist's head—scientific proof of the angel's presence. According to Bosworth, the holy agitation on Branham's left hand grew so intense in the presence of oppressing spirits that it would "stop his wrist watch instantly." After a spirit had been cast out, he added, one could visibly observe Branham's "red and swollen hand return to its normal condition."[11]

At the peak of his celebrity, however, erratic behavior began to undo him. Branham would cancel meetings or cut them short, pointing to some perceived defect in the crowd or the absence of the angel. He courted controversy with the denominations, slandering them as the "mark of the beast," and veered toward exotic doctrines and sensational claims. In a distant echo of John Dowie and Frank Sandford, he revealed himself to be the "End Time Messenger" who had come in the "spirit of Elijah," and disclosed that he would be empowered to transform saints into their glorified bodies prior to the Rapture. The seven angels of Revelation met him on Sunset Mountain in Arizona to commission the opening of the seven seals. By the 1960s, the dwindling number of his followers was matched only by their increasing devotion and loyalty. Most of them viewed their leader as at least the "prophet of Malachi 4," perhaps even Jesus Christ himself.[12]

When Branham died in a savage auto accident in December 1965, his most devout followers hoped to see his resurrection. They held his body in state for four months, ostensibly to allow his wife, also injured in the accident, to recover sufficiently to attend the burial. On April 11, 1966, after Easter had come and gone without event, the body of William Marrion Branham was finally interred.

Despite the irregularity of his later career, Branham would be remembered as the enigmatic mystic of deliverance evangelism, a holy man of legendary power whose meetings inspired unparalleled awe. He crossed the brightest line in Pentecostalism—that dividing the movement's Oneness from its Trinitarian stream—and did more than any other to launch healing evangelism to prominence in the early postwar years.

A. A. ALLEN

If Branham was the movement's soft-spoken seer, Asa Alonso Allen was its truculent warrior, ready to fight sin, Satan, and denominational officials at the drop of a hat. Like Branham, Allen was born in poverty to an alcoholic father, and, like Branham, he met an untimely death. But as a healing evangelist, he cut quite a different figure.

Converted at a Methodist meeting in 1934 at the age of 23, the Arkansas native quickly made his way into the AG, where, still in his mid-20s, he began a career as an evangelist and pastor. By 1947 he had taken charge of an AG congregation in Corpus Christi, Texas, but a settled ministry could hardly hold such a gifted and restless saint. In 1949 he attended an Oral Roberts crusade in Dallas and returned with hopes of starting his own radio program and healing ministry. When his congregation balked, Allen swapped the pulpit for the sawdust trail and never looked back. He purchased a large tent and set up headquarters in Dallas, where in short order he gained the radio program he had coveted and published *Miracle Magazine* to promote his new ministry.

Allen's maverick ways raised the hackles of AG leaders, and controversy followed him wherever he went. In 1955 Allen was arrested in Knoxville, Tennessee, for drunk driving, but when the AG sought to rein him in, he denied wrongdoing and surrendered his credentials rather than submit to ecclesiastical discipline. Thenceforth, Allen carried on a running skirmish with denominational Pentecostalism, and he gave as good as he got. Like Branham, he urged saints to trade the shackles of denominationalism for the liberty of independent Pentecost, pointing the way by founding his own Miracle Revival Fellowship in 1956.

Like other deliverance evangelists, Allen taught that miracles were only a means to a greater end—world evangelism; never shy of bombast, he once proclaimed "A Billion Souls Crusade." But miracles filled the tent, and no one bested Allen on that count. In the mid-1950s, "miracle oil" began to flow from the heads and hands of tent-meeting saints, and the recurring charism soon became an Allen trademark. Other signs abounded. On one occasion, a cross of blood appeared on his forehead; on another, a ball of fire rested over his tent. And that tent was one of the largest in the world after he purchased the mammoth 22,000-seat canvas that Jack Coe had used before his 1956 death.

Allen's miracles were often as graphic as they were grandiose: cancer patients coughed up their cancers into jars; demon-possessed men and women vomited out evil spirits. Furthermore, Allen was among the first to film these unsettling spectacles for all the television-viewing world to see. If Branham could raise the dead, Allen went one better, announcing a "raise the dead" program—he had to suspend it when credulous saints refused to bury their dearly departed. And Allen laid claim to some of the rarest cases of deliverance, as for example when a hermaphrodite reported divine gender reassignment. "God changed me completely to a male," he enthused. "Even my large breasts...vanished." Others noticed: "My boss says I go about my work now like a real man."[13]

Prosperity had always been a component of Allen's teaching, as seen in his 1953 *The Secret to Scriptural Financial Success*, and he had long hawked miracle merchandise like prayer cloths anointed with miracle oil and miracle tent shavings. But as deliverance evangelism became more competitive in the 1950s—and then lost steam—Allen shifted further toward the gospel of material provision.

In addition to the laws of faith and divine reciprocity, noted above, Allen stressed the "word of faith": the power to speak a thing into existence. One of his favorite tales recounted a time when God turned his one-dollar bills into twenties. "You don't have to believe it, because it doesn't have to happen to you," Allen rasped. "But it had to happen to me." He then shared the secret behind that miracle: "I decreed a thing," he explained. "God said 'Thou shall decree a thing, and it shall be established unto thee.'"

Allen stood ready and willing to apply his gift for the benefit of others: "I believe I can command God to perform a miracle for you financially," he asserted. After all, God wanted his followers to be wealthy. "I am a wealthy God!" he told Allen in 1963. "Claim my wealth in thy hand, yea, in thy purse." By that time, testimonies of financial deliverance had come to outnumber those of physical healing in *Miracle Magazine*.[14]

During the 1960s, the ground shifted for deliverance evangelism and successful practitioners had to adapt. Allen resisted, taking the mantle of old-fashioned revivalism in bold dissent to the more restrained, cultivated styles then taking hold. Yet, despite his rhetorical protest, he too changed with the times, adding Christian rock and "a little bit of the black beat" to better connect "with the Jesus kids."[15]

Trouble and controversy, though, had never lost Allen's scent, and they trailed him into the 1960s. Having lived separately from his wife for years, he scandalized supporters by divorcing her in 1967. The evangelist had waged a lifelong battle with the bottle—his personal demon. Now, the bottle gained the upper hand. In 1970, at the age of 59, Allen died in a San Francisco hotel. The coroner listed alcoholism as a contributing cause of death.

GRANVILLE ORAL ROBERTS

Of all the healing evangelists, Granville Oral Roberts rose to become by far the best known and most influential. His folksy yet professional demeanor made him the gentleman healer of deliverance evangelism, and both his longevity and the relative esteem afforded his ministry contrast sharply with the short, turbulent careers of Branham and Allen. Like other evangelists, Roberts possessed keen entrepreneurial drive and forged intimate connections with his followers. But unlike most, he had an uncanny knack for changing with the times, seamlessly reinventing deliverance evangelism for new generations without ever seeming to repudiate it.

Roberts was the son of an Oklahoma preacher affiliated with the Pentecostal Holiness Church. He began his career in 1936, at the age of 18, and soon won recognition as a rising star within his denomination. After a decade of evangelism and pastoral ministry, Roberts moved to Tulsa, where in a single pivotal year, 1947, he founded Healing Waters Revival Ministry (later Oral Roberts Evangelistic Association), launched a radio ministry, published a monthly magazine, *Healing Waters*, and wrote his first book, *If You Need Healing—Do These Things!* Roberts had a knack for promotion, crisscrossing the nation in a canvas cathedral billed as the largest gospel tent in the world, and he skyrocketed to fame. By the mid-1950s, he had become the nation's greatest disseminator of "full gospel" teaching.

Roberts distinguished himself in several ways within the field of deliverance. He adopted a trademark healing line in which hundreds of seekers passed by, single file, while he laid hands on each and every one of them. The divine mechanics of his healing power, furthermore, was Branhamesque, but with a twist: Each identified demons and diseases through vibrations of the hand, but where the sacred agitations worked on Branham's left, Roberts felt them in his right. In addition, Roberts broke his message into clear, logical principles, as with his "six simple steps" to healing, placing him in a tradition of rational revivalism running from Charles Finney's "new methods" to Bill Bright's "Four Spiritual Laws." Finally, although Roberts equaled his rivals as a healer, compiling an ample portfolio of cancers dissolved, blind eyes opened, and withered limbs extended, his crusades were models of decorum when judged by the norms of mid-century deliverance, which made them accessible to middle-class and non-Pentecostal visitors.

Known for his moderation and diplomacy, Roberts outstripped his contemporaries in the courtship of pastoral and denominational support. By the 1950s, moreover, he had turned those considerable skills to ecumenical ends, cultivating ties with mainline Protestants and even lay Catholics. As noted, all evangelists felt the ecumenical imperative to some degree, since they hoped to attract attendance from a broad cross-section of the population. But Roberts's genius lay in his ability to widen his appeal without fatally alienating his original constituency.

As the deliverance trade changed, Roberts made subtle adjustments that slowly reshaped his ministry, gravitating away from big-top healing and toward evangelism and prosperity teaching. The latter in particular marked the way of the future. Roberts's preaching and his public appeals increasingly centered on wholeness and happiness—God's gift of the good life—and in 1956 he changed the title of his periodical accordingly, to *Abundant Life*. Roberts elaborated the laws of faith into a "blessing pact"—more fully developed later as the doctrine of "seed faith"—declaring that God would return gifts to his ministry "seven fold." So confident was Roberts in the operation of this law that he offered a money-back guarantee, promising to refund any donations that had not, within a year's time, been miraculously repaid in full. *Abundant Life* brimmed with testimonies of contributions made and blessings duly received.

Tactics of this kind fell within the norms of deliverance fundraising, where evangelists jostled for donors by touting special benefits or blessings sure to follow any contribution. Alternately, evangelists appealed to the business sense of contributors, stressing the heavenly return on investment as measured in soul-winning efficiency. A common gimmick was to quantify performance, as when Allen boasted of souls at "twenty-five cents each, or FOUR FOR A DOLLAR!"[16] Here also, Roberts found innovative ways to change the game. In addition to mass appeals, he held business luncheons and cultivated "partners," well-heeled backers whose reliable support he repaid with exclusive conferences and access to the inner circles of his ministry.

In the late 1950s and early 1960s, deliverance hit hard times. A new cultural mood rendered the old style less relevant—some said obsolete—and exposés like one published in 1962 by insider Granville Harrison portrayed a movement rife with fraud, financial chicanery, and outrageous claims. The movement began to fray. Lindsay's *Voice of Healing*, for example, had evolved into a loose association of revivalists who agreed to abide by certain guidelines, thus imposing a degree of regularity on the movement. At its peak in the mid-1950s, more than 100 evangelists had gathered under its canopy. A short decade later, little sign of that cohesion remained. Lindsay himself had moved on, and the World Convention of Deliverance Evangelists, which had attempted to fill his place, folded its tent in 1965 after a seven-year run.

Faced with these changing circumstances, Roberts took decisive steps to mold a more sophisticated persona and fashion a ministry capable of thriving at the heart of mainstream popular culture. In 1965, he burnished his reputation by founding Oral Roberts University in Tulsa, and then persuaded America's most respected Protestant Christian, Billy Graham, to deliver its dedication address. In 1968, Roberts affiliated with the United Methodist Church, though he assured Pentecostals that his original beliefs and practices still held firm. As important as these steps may have been, however, television provided the vehicle that carried Roberts above the ruins of old-time deliverance and on to new heights of success.

Roberts had broken fresh ground in many areas of deliverance evangelism, but he simply revolutionized its use of television. Only 5 percent of U.S. homes had televisions in 1950. Ten years later, that figure had climbed to one-half. Evangelists like Roberts, Allen, and Rex Humbard readily perceived the extraordinary potential of the new medium, but television was problematic for Pentecostals. Because it closely resembled "moving pictures," a traditional taboo, most saints had condemned the new contraptions. Nevertheless, the evangelists pressed forward.

Roberts's first foray into television programming, in 1954, involved filming crusades for television rebroadcast, hoping to transport the atmosphere of those meetings into the living rooms of his viewers. His perfectionist temperament and inventive mind, however, drove him beyond these rudimentary beginnings. Roberts quickly recognized the need to shape his content to fit the new format. Furthermore, he aspired to the highest professional standards of achievement. After considerable experimentation, Roberts found his formula. Using state-of-the-art production equipment, he developed a crisp, syndicated weekly show that rivaled the best secular programming in quality of production. It became the leading religious program in the nation.

In 1968, recognizing that television had replaced the tent meeting as the cornerstone of his ministry, Roberts retired from the deliverance circuit, trading the big top for the television studio. Even then, he did not stand still. Roberts supplemented his weekly program—now called *Oral Roberts Presents*—with slickly produced quarterly specials filmed at NBC studios in Burbank, California. Featuring Oral Roberts University's modish World Action Singers and celebrity guests like Mahalia Jackson, Pat Boone, Roy Rogers, and Jerry Lewis, the specials were a resounding hit, drawing television audiences in the tens of millions. And whether tuning in to his specials or to his weekly program, viewers found the same upbeat message. "God is a good God," became his signature refrain. "Something good," Roberts soothingly intoned, "is going to happen to you!"

By the mid-1970s, Roberts had made the transition from tent-meeting evangelist to chief executive officer of a multimedia empire. His university had plans for graduate programs in law, business, education, and other fields. A massive City of Faith Medical and Research Center loomed just ahead. Arrayed behind him were 800,000 prayer partners. The circulation of *Abundant Life* had passed one million, and his combined ministries generated annual revenue of $15 million. Now, a new generation stood in the wings: Morris Cerullo, who best mirrored Roberts's own professional style; Jim Bakker, pioneering the Christian variety show; and the enormously talented Jimmy Swaggart, refitting old-time revivalism to the electronic age. But with his genial charm and avuncular bearing, Oral Roberts still towered as the grand old man of televangelism, the phenomenon that he had done more than anyone to create. As much at ease in the 1970s as he had been 30 years before, Roberts had years of success and celebrity yet ahead of him.[17]

INDEPENDENT PENTECOSTALISM

Postwar revitalization movements, as noted, fueled the growth of independent Pentecostalism. Animated by the New Order of the Latter Rain and the boisterous breezes of deliverance, a stream of congregations, ministries, and small associations of kindred free spirits poured into the open spaces of Pentecostalism. But "independence" hardly conveys the true picture, since many of the leading agencies and actors continued to work effectively in and among denominational circles. To a great extent, then, independent Pentecostalism served a parachurch function, bridging and blurring the old boundaries.

The Full Gospel Business Men's Fellowship International (FGBMFI), founded in 1951 by wealthy California dairyman, Demos Shakarian, offers a good illustration. Organized on the advice of Oral Roberts, whose 1951 Los Angeles crusade Shakarian had helped to bankroll, the FGBMFI began as a forum in which Spirit-filled businessmen could meet for mutual encouragement. From its inception, the fellowship had close ties to deliverance evangelism—its early speakers were a who's who of the movement—but it soon cast its net much wider. Within a few short years, the FGBMFI had developed into a leading venue for the introduction of Pentecostal spirituality to the mainline world, as full gospel clergy and businessmen of all denominations and none invited friends and associates to nonsectarian gatherings at restaurants, hotel ballrooms, and other upscale spots to share their Holy Ghost experiences. By the mid-1960s, it had expanded to 300 chapters and 100,000 members nationwide, and its monthly magazine, *Full Gospel Business Men's Voice*, teemed with testimonials from mainstream Christians who had encountered the power of Pentecost.

The later career of Gordon Lindsay provides another example. By the 1960s, Lindsay had migrated "out of the world of tents and shouting and into a world of...thoughtful evangelism."[18] Foreign missions became his vital interest, where he worked to develop indigenous leadership on the model of evangelist T. L. Osborn's Association for Native Evangelism. In 1963 he joined with independents like J. C. Hibbard—radio evangelist and pastor of the Gospel Lighthouse, a Dallas, Texas, megachurch—to organize the Full Gospel Fellowship of Churches and Ministers International. Four years later, he reorganized his several ministries into Christ for the Nations, Inc., headquartered in Dallas, and in 1970 opened a missionary training center, Christ for the Nations Institute. Although Lindsay surrendered his AG credentials in 1965, he continued to maintain good relations with his former denomination, and Christ for the Nations served a constituency that included both denominational and independent Pentecostals along with full gospel believers in the mainline churches.

Postwar revitalization movements made their greatest contribution by creating zones of syncretistic interface of precisely this kind, bringing together groups and individuals from across the Pentecostal spectrum. Furthermore, since many independents did not share denominational Pentecostalism's scruples against fraternizing with mainliners and Catholics, they invited them into this fertile melding ground as well. Often, they followed the lead of David du Plessis by urging Pentecostalized mainliners to work for renewal within their own denominations rather than join an openly Pentecostal body. In these and other ways, independent Pentecostalism helped create the preconditions for the Charismatic Renewal: a dynamic eruption of Pentecostal phenomena within mainline Protestant denominations and the Roman Catholic Church, which many rank as the single most important development in 20th-century world Christianity.

THE CHARISMATIC MOVEMENT

Throughout the postwar years, the core elements of a Pentecostal worldview filtered into mainline churches along various conduits. In addition to healing evangelism and independent organizations like the FGBMFI, the National Association of Evangelicals brought Pentecostal leaders into contact with wary evangelicals, while du Plessis cultivated friendships in ecumenical circles. A less visible but equally important conduit flowed from the assiduous commitment of individual Pentecostals—clergy and laity alike—to proselytize their friends, neighbors, and associates. As a result, most mainline denominations had at least some Pentecostal presence by the 1950s, including Agnes Sanford and Richard Winkler (Episcopalian); Harald Bredeson (Lutheran); Gerald Derstine (Mennonite); James Brown, (Presbyterian); Tommy Tyson (United Methodist); John Osteen and Pat Robertson (Southern Baptist); and Howard Ervin (American Baptist). Although most nurtured their experience quietly to avoid controversy, Spirit-filled mainliners found acceptance in mainline healing or spiritual formation ministries like the Order of St. Luke and Camps Farthest Out.

The surprising infiltration of Pentecostal spirituality into mainline churches, however, did not hit the headlines until 1960. Over the previous year, dozens of Episcopal laypersons in suburban Los Angeles, together with a few of their priests, had received Holy Spirit baptism and had spoken in tongues. The group included John and Joan Baker and parish priest Frank McGuire of Holy Spirit Parish in Monterey Park, along with Jean Stone (later Jean Stone Willans) and Rector Dennis Bennett of St. Mark's Episcopal Church in Van Nuys. When Bennett publicly announced his experience in April 1960, a firestorm erupted. Rather than fuel controversy, Bennett resigned his pastorate, transferring to Seattle, where he took the helm of St. Luke's Episcopal Church and transformed it into a key center of the novel phenomenon.

Meanwhile, back in Van Nuys, Stone had taken matters into her own capable hands, alerting *Time* and *Newsweek* to the curious and contentious affair. Both magazines recognized a story when they heard one, and the articles they published that summer sparked a national sensation, bringing public awareness of, and internal self-consciousness to, the incipient movement. In the months ahead, Stone and her associates took steps to nurture the outpouring by establishing the Blessed Trinity Society, with du Plessis and Bredeson on its board of directors, and by publishing a quarterly journal, *Trinity*.

Journalists and scholars first dubbed the phenomenon the new Pentecostalism, or neo-Pentecostalism. But insiders like Stone and Bredeson preferred other self-ascriptions—the charismatic movement, or the charismatic renewal—and those terms eventually won out. The altered landscape dictated new terminology for Pentecostalism proper as well, which, following the suggestion of Catholic scholar Kilian McDonnell, came to be known as classical Pentecostalism.

Over the next decade, the charismatic movement birthed a flourishing network of leaders, retreat centers, organizations, and publications, with active renewal societies in every denominational family in the United States. The more prominent leaders and societies included George "Brick" Bradford and J. Rodman Williams of the Charismatic Communion of Presbyterian Ministers, later Presbyterian Charismatic Communion; Bennett and Graham Pulkingham of the Episcopal Charismatic Fellowship; and Larry Christenson of the Lutheran Charismatic Renewal Services. The renewal stirred dissension among mainstream Protestant denominations, and virtually all conducted studies to assess it. In the end, however, only more fundamentalist bodies like the Southern Baptist Convention, the Church of the Nazarene, and the Lutheran Church, Missouri Synod failed to extend at least cautious approval to the movement.

While the charismatic movement spread through mainline Protestant circles, devotional currents like the Cursillo movement merged with the epochal transformations unleashed by the Second Vatican Council to revitalize Catholic piety. The council had endorsed greater lay participation, ecumenical exchange, and innovations in worship and had also affirmed the validity and importance of charismatic gifts. Indeed, Pope John had voiced hope that the council might occasion a "new Pentecost" for the Catholic Church.

In 1967, two years after the conclusion of Vatican II, that papal hope seemed to meet its fulfillment when charismatic renewal sprang to life on the campuses of four Midwestern universities. The events began at Duquesne University in Pittsburgh, where lay faculty who had studied books by David Wilkerson (Pentecostal) and John Sherrill (charismatic) experienced Spirit-baptism and spoke in tongues. They subsequently convened a religious retreat at which several students were introduced to the experience. News of charismatic empowerment shot through Catholic student and faculty networks, and similar manifestations erupted at Notre Dame, Michigan State, and the University of Michigan. Just as at Van Nuys, moreover, the jarring novelty of these events drew the glare of media spotlights and caused a national sensation.

The university setting provided ideal conditions for disseminating the movement, connecting zealous advocates of renewal to national circuits of student, academic, and parish life, and charismatic renewal grew at a dizzying pace. Within months, a national conference convened at Notre Dame, and lay-oriented "covenant communities" soon sprang up. These included the Word of God community in Ann Arbor, Michigan, led by Stephen Clark and Ralph Martin; People of Praise in South Bend, Indiana, led by Kevin Ranaghan; Mother of God in Gaithersburg, Maryland, led by Judith Tydings and Edith Defato; and Alleluia community in Augusta, Georgia, led by Dale Clark and Bill Beatty. In 1970, the communities at Ann Arbor and South Bend organized Charismatic Renewal Services and the National Service Committee to supply resources and bring cohesion to the movement. A publication, *New Covenant,* appeared the following year. In 1974, less than a decade after the movement's inception, a Catholic charismatic renewal conference at Notre Dame drew 30,000 attendees. By that time, scores of regional and diocesan renewal centers, teaching and healing ministries, and charismatic conferences had emerged to serve the now global phenomenon.[19]

UNITY AND DIFFERENCE

Common themes, emphases, and behaviors lent broad continuity across the Pentecostal-charismatic spectrum. All quarters resonated with the ancient restorationist refrain, seeking to recover the purity and power of early Christianity. Similar patterns of praise worship provided another common denominator. This generally included collective supplication to or magnification of God, aided by repetitive choruses or prayerful meditation that induced a feeling of intense communion with the Holy. The raising of hands and the use of contemporary instrumental music were also pervasive, along with ecstatic manifestations ranging from quiet, trancelike states and varieties of glossolalia to exuberant outbursts of weeping, laughing, dancing, and being "slain in spirit."

In addition, all parts of the Pentecostal-charismatic world expressed devotion to the authority of the Bible and shared a sacred worldview in which the signs, wonders, gifts, and offices related in Scripture remained as valid for their own day as for the days of the saints and apostles. Consequently, Spirit-baptized Christians of all kinds accepted the reality of the dark as well as the light side of the supernatural: spiritual warfare against evil forces constituted the flip side of spiritual gifts and empowerment. Most groups also shared a millenarian or quasi-millenarian hope for the soon coming of Jesus Christ. Finally, all were infused with profound missionary fervor, a keen desire to spread the good news of Holy Ghost renewal.

Yet significant differences remained, etching lines of demarcation and raising impediments to fellowship between charismatics and classical Pentecostals. As a general rule, charismatics held historic Christian traditions in higher regard than did either denominational or independent Pentecostals. Moreover, charismatic leaders often felt more comfortable with scholarly theological discourse than did their Pentecostal peers. Correspondingly, their ranks included a greater number of highly trained scholars, such as Erwin, Williams, and Catholics like Donald Gelpi and Peter Hocken.

In addition, virtually all charismatics stressed that glossolalia was but one of the spiritual gifts—*a* sign of Spirit baptism, not *the* sign—thus demoting it from its privileged position in classical Pentecostalism. Since most classical Pentecostals still held mainliners and Roman Catholics in suspicion, the charismatic breach on "initial evidence" raised doubts about the movement's capacity for doctrinal soundness. This difference loomed especially large for classical Pentecostal theologians because it implicitly questioned Pentecostalism's reason for existing as a separate movement.

Perhaps the sharpest rift, however, rose imperceptibly from subtle patterns of gesture, comportment, and expression that ultimately rested on the deep structures of class and socialization. In many respects, classical Pentecostalism still echoed the rough-and-ready disposition of its plainfolk roots. Charismatic worship, on the other hand, called to mind adjectives like *gentle* and *dignified.* Among charismatics, that is to say, glossolalia tripped from the lips in an upper-middle-class accent.

At first, then, classical Pentecostals were slow to affirm the charismatic movement, which some of them scorned as "the cruisamatics." Those sentiments, to be sure, were rather mutual, which is precisely why charismatics like Stone and Bredeson flinched at the moniker, neo-Pentecostal. According to Sherrill, charismatics felt caught between "the uncouth life of the Pentecostals and the aesthetic death of the older churches."[20]

Yet the links between Pentecostals and charismatics remained undeniable. "Behind every early charismatic," observed McDonnell, "stood a classical Pentecostal."[21] And whatever the misgivings of denominational leaders and plainfolk saints, scores of classical Pentecostal clergy and parachurch organizations rose to encourage and partner with the new movement. Ralph Wilkerson's Melodyland Christian Center, Loren Cunningham's Youth With A Mission, Stephen Strang's *Charisma,* and many others openly embraced charismatics.

By the mid-1970s, collaboration between classical Pentecostals and charismatics had become so tightly interwoven in some ministries and organizations that it was impossible to trace the boundary between them. In 1971, Dan Malachuk, a Pentecostal reared in New York's historic Glad Tidings Tabernacle, acquired *Herald of Faith, Harvest Time* magazine (itself a merger of the Pentecostal Joseph Mattsson-Boze's *Herald of Faith* and the charismatic Gerald Derstine's *Harvest Time,* both heavily influenced by the New Order of the Latter Rain). Malachuk renamed it *Logos Journal,* and turned it into the leading periodical for the charismatic movement. In Fort Lauderdale, Florida, Don Basham (Disciples of Christ) and Charles Simpson (Southern Baptist) joined three men with classical Pentecostal roots—Bob Mumford, Derek Prince, and Ern Baxter—to launch Christian Growth Ministries and a discipleship movement that would vex and inspire charismatics for years to come.

The list of liminal zones could be extended almost indefinitely: the FGBMFI and its counterpart, Women's Aglow; Pat Robertson's Christian Broadcasting Network; the healing campaigns of Kathryn Kuhlman; the campus of Oral Roberts University. But nothing better illustrated the creative syncretism bursting from the interstices of the Pentecostal world than did the "Jesus People Movement,"

a vibrant response to the counterculture that hit the scene in the late
1960s.

THE JESUS PEOPLE MOVEMENT

By the mid-1960s, complex reactions against mainstream culture
had begun to coalesce into a powerful youth movement known as the
counterculture. The Sixties counterculture, admittedly, owed much to
1950s youth creativity and discontent: rock 'n' roll, beatnik philosophy,
drug experimentation, and political turmoil surrounding the early
civil rights movement. But the counterculture truly galvanized around
alienation caused by the Vietnam War, civil rights violence, and repres-
sion of the counterculture itself. Buoyed by the rising share of youth in
post–baby boom America, the counterculture lashed out at the existing establishment and sought to embody a visionary alternative to the
previous generation's way of life.

Though hardly a united movement, most expressions of the counterculture traced to the pursuit of a few core values, such as authenticity, freedom, self-realization, and community. Americans in the
counterculture felt that their parents' generation had utterly failed to
realize those values, leaving them to come of age in a society marked by
shallow commercialism, violence, racism, class pretension, and moral
codes that were as hypocritical as they were repressive. One response
was negative: simply to reject everything that was considered phony,
stale, or corrupt about the inherited past. But the counterculture developed positive responses as well. In true primitivist fashion, activists
sought to strip the core elements of culture to their essence, and then
to create de novo their own art, literature, music, philosophy, fashion,
religion, and politics. Above all, they wished to create forms of community marked by love, cooperation, and mutual affirmation rather
than competitive self-aggrandizement.

There is some truth to the view that sex, drugs, and rock 'n' roll
constituted the sacraments of the counterculture. Sexual intercourse,
particularly in light of the new birth control pill, could be celebrated
as a revolutionary act of love, self-expression, and liberation from
Victorian strictures. The use of drugs like marijuana and the experi-
mental hallucinogen, LSD, served as both emblems and rites of
passage, initiating newcomers and conveying symbolic evidence of
one's commitment to peace, love, and understanding. Furthermore,
drugs were promoted by gurus like Timothy Leary as pathways to
enlightenment. And music may have provided the strongest element
of cohesion for the counterculture; the movement's largest collective

gatherings occurred at music festivals like the Monterey International Pop Festival in 1967 and, most famously, the 1969 Woodstock Music and Art Fair held near Bethel, New York.

Hippies and flower children viewed themselves as a beneficent presence, indeed, as avatars of a coming Age of Aquarius. But their behavior sparked outrage and alarm among conservative Americans. Many Pentecostals and evangelicals, though, reacted differently. Where others saw subversion, they saw an opportunity to reach a generation for Christ.

The counterculture did in fact offer intriguing prospects for evangelism. It reflected a generational search for meaning and thirsted for purity and authenticity. Furthermore, religious and philosophical reflection within the movement already showed deep interest in Jesus as a countercultural archetype. Finally, troubling needs and hardships lay just beneath the movement's ebullient surface. Lofty ideals and pockets of utopia contrasted sharply with the reality of life on the streets, where young men and women—often homeless runaways—faced the encroaching threats of poverty, sickness, drug addiction, unwanted pregnancy, and exploitation.

Though by no means an exclusively Pentecostal affair, Pentecostals stepped to the fore of this outreach, drawing on their rich heritage of ministry at the social margins and among the down and out. Acknowledging the countercultural posture of Jesus in his own time, they wove the music, styles, and even much of the value system of the counterculture into a powerfully appealing expression of Christianity. Youth were urged to "get high on Jesus," with Spirit baptism and Pentecostal worship as the peak experiences that could transport one to true enlightenment.

Jesus People, however, were as drawn to authentic community as they were to authentic experience, and outreach ministries provided just this through congregations and fellowship groups bound together by love and mutual accountability. Within a few short years, scores of congregations had made the Jesus People their object of focus, while hundreds of Jesus communes beckoned those who desired the discipline and devotion of a vocational life.

As with the counterculture itself, music doubled as both drawing card and social adhesive for the Jesus People movement. Pentecostalism had always been musically adaptive, quick to employ up-tempo honky-tonk beats, country and bluegrass styles, and popular instrumentation to draw and hold a crowd. Indeed, Pentecostalism had become a veritable training ground for popular artists, exerting a formative influence on secular stars ranging from Johnny Cash, Tammy

Wynette, and Jerry Lee Lewis to Little Richard, B. B. King, and Elvis
Presley. The Jesus People likewise spawned a rich musical culture,
pouring Christian motifs through folk and hard rock melodies. Youth
streamed into Christian coffee houses, church sanctuaries, and public
auditoriums to worship to the audacious strains of gospel rock pio-
neers like Larry Norman, Phil Keaggy, and Chuck Girard. In the
process, Christian contemporary music was born.

Arguably, the most important Pentecostal contribution to the Jesus
People movement traced to the labors of David Wilkerson, an AG
pastor who had embarked on a street ministry among New York
City gang members in the 1950s. Toward the end of that decade, he
established an organization called Teen Challenge to recruit and train
Christian youth for urban evangelism and to provide Spirit-filled
treatment for the alcoholism and drug addiction so rampant among
his converts. Over the next several years, Wilkerson opened an
extensive network of Teen Challenge training and rehabilitation centers. Wilkerson told his story in *The Cross and the Switchblade* (1963),
a best-seller that inspired scores of imitators and did more than any
book of its time to spread the Pentecostal message beyond the borders
of Pentecostalism. When the Jesus People emerged in the late 1960s,
Teen Challenge personnel like Nicky Cruz, author of *Run, Baby, Run*
(1968); Linda Meissner, head of the Jesus People Army; and Sonny
Arguinzoni, founder of the East Los Angeles–based Victory Outreach,
were already on the scene.

The International Church of the Foursquare Gospel and its offshoots
also made vital contributions to the Jesus People movement. In the
early 1960s, an independent-minded ex-Foursquare pastor, Charles
"Chuck" Smith, took charge of a small congregation in Costa Mesa
called Calvary Chapel. Smith directed his attention to the hippies and
beach bums of Costa Mesa, establishing a network of "Jesus houses"
where homeless youth could find shelter and Christian nurture. A
turning point came when Smith met a dynamic young "Jesus freak,"
Lonnie Frisbee, who had worked among Jesus People in Haight-
Ashbury. Frisbee possessed a striking capacity to draw countercultural
youth to Christianity, and with Frisbee leading its midweek Bible
study, Calvary Chapel exploded from perhaps 200 members to over
2,000 within a matter of months.

Smith also entrusted Frisbee and John Higgins with a communal home known as the House of Miracles. Under their leadership it
spawned a score of duplicate homes and laid the foundation for Shiloh
Youth Revival Centers, the largest network of communes in the Jesus
People movement. Although Smith permitted Pentecostal distinctives

like glossolalia, he did not emphasize them. Frisbee and others, however, placed them front and center, and their influence shaped the spirituality of the new movement.

Within the Foursquare proper, Ralph Moore took charge of Hope Chapel in 1971, a struggling congregation in the South Bay area of Los Angeles. Moore targeted young singles by blanketing his neighborhood with free copies of Wilkerson's *Cross and the Switchblade*, and the response was overwhelming. Hope Chapel grew exponentially, spinning off satellite congregations and joining another classical Pentecostal body, Bethel Tabernacle in nearby Redondo Beach, as key centers of the Jesus People movement.

The Jesus People also drew the attention of Pentecostal healing evangelists. As noted above, A. A. Allen and Oral Roberts adopted more youthful styles of music and dress to better relate to the new generation. But the leading outreach came from T. L. Osborn, an evangelist with Pentecostal Church of God roots whose greatest success had occurred overseas. Between 1968 and 1972, he shifted his emphasis from foreign missions to the youth of America, growing out his hair, donning hip fashions, and conducting well-attended youth rallies across the country.

Many traditionalists, to be sure, never accepted the Jesus People. They simply could not reconcile bare feet, long hair, outlandish dress, and hippie music with their concept of Christianity. But in reality, countercultural survivals within the Jesus People movement proved to be rather superficial. By and large, it steered former hippies and flower children back toward conservative social values and religious assumptions—that is, toward biblical literalism in the tone, dialect, and dress of the counterculture.

A movement so complex—indeed inchoate—could hardly be credited to a single source. Yet, like the charismatic movement before it, the Jesus People movement attested to the growing ability of Pentecostalism to influence its wider culture. In its frank supernaturalism, its primitivist urge to restore apostolic Christianity, its millenarian expectation, and its Spirit-centered openness to tongues, healing, and other charismatic gifts, the Jesus People movement bore the telltale imprint of Pentecostalism.

THE ENGINE OF PENTECOSTALISM

The creative dynamism of Pentecostalism may have flourished best in the cross-pollinating margins of the movement, but the denominations remained its driving force. Indeed, as we have seen, they formed the wellspring of those revitalizing currents that overspilled their borders. Furthermore, the routinization decried by purists played an invaluable role in the movement's success. The postwar bureaucratic model offered far more than a bulwark against abuses or a guarantee of brand identity. It enabled long-range planning, efficient application of collective effort, and continuity over time.

The results spoke for themselves. By 1955, the AG had reached 400,000 in membership. Fifteen years later, that figure topped 600,000, with growth among Hispanic districts leading the way. Among other Finished Work Pentecostals, the International Church of the Foursquare Gospel passed 200,000 adherents in the 1970s, with the Pentecostal Church of God not far behind.

The Church of God in Christ stood at the fore of Holiness Pentecostalism, reporting more than 400,000 members by the mid-1960s. This reflected Pentecostalism's extraordinary gains in African American communities across the nation: surveys indicated that 5 percent of black Americans were Pentecostal by the mid-1960s, as opposed to only 2 percent of whites. The Church of God (Cleveland, Tennessee) placed a close second in the Holiness field. Its membership had more than doubled between 1944 and 1954, from 67,000 to 138,000. Twenty years later, it had more than doubled again, reaching 320,000 in 1974. The Pentecostal Holiness Church grew more slowly than its peers but still topped 70,000 in 1970. As an indication of its expanding reach and vision—and perhaps also of the importance of its most famous scion, Oral Roberts—the body moved its headquarters from Franklin Springs, Georgia, to Oklahoma City in 1974. As these figures suggest, Pentecostalism grew with special vigor in the Holiness-dominated South, which, by the mid-1960s, claimed more than a million Pentecostals.

Oneness Pentecostals experienced rapid growth as well, with the largest body, the United Pentecostal Church, cresting 100,000 members by 1970, followed by the Pentecostal Assemblies of the World with a membership of 45,000. Additional thousands gathered in scores of smaller bodies, including the Apostolic Assembly of Faith in Christ Jesus, which expanded geographically as well as numerically throughout the period, and upstarts like the Bible Way Churches of Our Lord Jesus Christ World Wide, established by Smallwood Williams in 1957 as a break from the Church of Our Lord Jesus Christ of the Apostolic Faith.

By the early 1970s, an estimated four million Americans filled the pews and folding chairs of Pentecostal churches across the United States, their growth in adherence matched or exceeded by increases in revenue and assets.

As it had been from the beginning, moreover, American Pentecostalism existed in symbiosis with missionary affiliates and autonomous Pentecostal bodies overseas. Building on prior generations of missionary effort, Pentecostal denominations combined their organizational and funding prowess with the missionary zeal of their members to promote the astounding growth of the movement in Latin America, Africa, and Asia. Perhaps aided by its frankly supernatural worldview, Pentecostalism demonstrated an uncanny ability to convey the power and purpose of a transformed life in terms that were relevant and intelligible across cultures. American Pentecostals, moreover, placed increasing stress on indigenization, cultivating "national pastors" for their missionary endeavors and effecting organizational unions with indigenous denominations overseas. In Korea, for example, an AG convert, Paul Yonggi Cho, founded the Yoido Full Gospel Church in Seoul, which grew to become the largest Christian congregation in the world. By the 1970s, the growth of Pentecostalism abroad had far outstripped that in the United States, with surveyors counting from 12 million to as many as 50 million Pentecostals worldwide.[22]

CONCLUSION

John Updike famously claimed that the 1950s ended in 1963, when "Lee Harvey Oswald shot them dead."[23] Perhaps. But for the 1960s, there would be no definitive end. Watergate and the conclusion of the Vietnam War are often given as terminus points, but neither was an event as such. The war staggered toward an ambiguous ending for years before the last ground troops trickled home in 1973, and personnel remained until the ignominious fall of Saigon two years later. And though Watergate may have dealt the deathblow to Sixties idealism, that too was a slow strangulation by degrees. The scandal dragged on through 1973 and still lingered after Nixon's resignation in August 1974.

But whatever date we place on the epitaph of the 1960s, the era witnessed the transformation of American Pentecostalism. Its long denouement lifted to reveal a new, less oppositional, but organizationally and numerically stronger movement, one forged in the clash between its own internal dynamics and postwar changes that had crested in the thrilling turbulence of the Sixties. With a phalanx of strong institutions leading the way, Pentecostals had made their progression from separation to social influence. Now, open before them, lay yet greater prospects. A seat at the table, the right to be heard, their fair share of, not merely influence, but political power: for many Pentecostals, these were no more than what their collective wealth and numbers said they rightfully deserved.

NOTES

1. Daniel Ramiriz, "Antonio Castañeda Nava: Charisma, Culture, and Caudillismo," in *Portraits of a Generation,* eds. James Goff, Jr. and Grant Wacker (Fayetteville: University of Arkansas Press, 2002), 304.

2. "All the nations": I Samuel 8, where the people of Israel petition for a king, a text often used against efforts to conform to mainstream social norms; for Assemblies of God higher education, see Gary B. McGee, *People of the Spirit: The Assemblies of God* (Springfield, MO: Gospel Publishing House, 2004), 333–335; and Edith Blumhofer, *Restoring the Faith: The Assemblies of God, Pentecostalism, and American Culture* (Urbana: University of Illinois Press, 1993), 254.

3. John Thomas Nichol, *Pentecostalism* (New York: Harper & Row, 1966), 229. A more gentle shepherd might have called diplomatically for a hymn.

4. Lesslie Newbigin, *The Household of God* (London: SCM Press, 1953); Henry P. Van Dusen, "The Third Force," *Life,* June 9, 1958; *Time,* November 2, 1962, quoted in Nichol, 245; du Plessis quoted in Blumhofer, *Restoring the Faith,* 233.

5. Blumhofer, *Restoring the Faith,* 232, 243.

6. Nichol, 221.

7. See Blumhofer, *Restoring the Faith,* 204–211; Vinson Synan, *The Holiness-Pentecostal Tradition: Charismatic Movements in the Twentieth Century,* rev. ed. (Grand Rapids, MI: Wm. B. Eerdmans Publishing, 1997), 212–213; and R. M. Riss, "Latter Rain Movement," in *The New International Dictionary of Pentecostal and Charismatic Movements,* rev. and exp. ed., eds. Stanley Burgess and Eduard van der Mass (Grand Rapids, MI: Zondervan, 2003), 830–833.

8. Key proof-texts included John 13–14: "And whatsoever ye shall ask in my name, that will I do....If ye shall ask any thing in my name, I will do it"; Matthew 21:22: "And all things, whatsoever ye shall ask in prayer, believing, ye shall receive"; Luke 6:38: "Give, and it shall be given unto you: good measure, pressed down, and shaken together, and running over, shall men give into your bosom"; and Malachi 3:10: "Bring ye all the tithes into the storehouse...and prove me now herewith...if I will not open you the windows of heaven, and pour you out a blessing, that there shall not be room enough to receive it."

9. My account of the postwar deliverance evangelists relies on Edwin Harrell, Jr., *All Things Are Possible: The Healing and Charismatic Revivals in Modern America* (Bloomington: Indiana University Press, 1975). On prewar healing evangelism, see Grant Wacker, *Heaven Below: Early Pentecostals and American Culture* (Cambridge, MA: Harvard University Press, 2001), 26.

10. TV and immortality: O. L. Jaggars; demons: W. V. Grant; body-felt salvation: Franklin Hall, in Harrell, *All Things Are Possible,* 79, 88, 212–213, respectively.

11. Harrell, 37.

12. Harrell, 165.

13. Harrell, 199.

14. Harrell, 75, 200–201. "Thou shalt decree" is Job 22:28.

15. Harrell, 196.

16. Allen, *Your Christian Dollar* (1958), quoted in Harrell, 104–105.

17. For more on Roberts, see Harrell, *Oral Roberts: An American Life* (Bloomington: Indiana University Press, 1985).

18. Harrell, *All Things Are Possible,* 167.

19. For the charismatic movement, see Peter D. Hocken, "Charismatic Movement," in Burgess and van der Maas, 477–519; and Richard Quebedeaux, *The New Charismatics II* (New York: Harper & Row, 1983).

20. John Sherrill, *They Speak with Other Tongues,* 162, quoted in Harrell, *All Things Are Possible,* 232.

21. Quoted in Vinson Synan, *The Century of the Holy Spirit: 100 Years of Pentecostal and Charismatic Renewal, 1901–2001* (Nashville, TN: Thomas Nelson, 2001), 213.

22. Statistics are drawn from relevant sections of Synan, *The Holiness-Pentecostal Tradition,* and *Century of the Holy Spirit;* McGee, *People of the Spirit;* Burgess and van der Mass, *The New International Dictionary;* Margaret Poloma, *The Assemblies of God at the Crossroads: Charisma and Institutional Dilemmas* (Knoxville: University of Tennessee Press, 1989); Blumhofer, *Restoring the Faith;* Charles Conn, *Like a Mighty Army,* rev. ed. (Cleveland, TN: Pathway Press, 1977); and Mickey Crews, *The Church of God: A Social History* (Knoxville: University of Tennessee Press, 1990). For a survey of global Pentecostalism, see Allan Anderson, *An Introduction to Pentecostalism: Global Charismatic Christianity* (Cambridge: Cambridge University Press, 2004).

23. John Updike, *S: A Novel* (New York: Alfred A. Knopf, 1988), 15.

CHAPTER 5

A Mighty Host

As the 20th century gave way to the 21st, Pentecostalism's long trajectory of growth and change carried it to new heights of confidence and cultural standing. The erstwhile outcasts now made a home in their American Zion, nestling into one broad sector of an increasingly divided U.S. mainstream. Pentecostalism continued to expand, but growth within corollary movements it had helped to spawn accelerated at an even more rapid pace. In tandem with the charismatic movement, Pentecostalism now midwifed a third wave of renewal, as congregations and denominations across the United States and the world adopted key elements of the lively Pentecostal style while often stopping just short of practices like glossolalia. And nondenominational or postdenominational offshoots sprouted from the interstices of the Pentecostal and charismatic movements, creating a neo-charismatic analog within what had by then become a mighty host of Spirit-filled believers. Religious demographers coined a term—renewalists—to encompass these movements collectively, and despite the differences that divided them, a growing sense of shared interests, even a vague common identity, began to take root across much of that wide spectrum.

As had always been the case, the adaptable movement bent with the winds of time, though creatively so. As a consequence, Pentecostalism, in the course of its evolution, limned the history of the United States at large. In the wake of the turbulent Sixties, for example, the

nation lurched to the political center and center-right, though hardly
in unison. Simmering memories and continuing trends sharpened historic divides and fueled what came to be known as the culture wars:
a post-Sixties battle for the soul of America between starkly different
visions of the Good Society, with the nation's not-always-silent majority stranded in poorly marked terrain between the extremes. The
grand campaigns became more focused, less systemic: feminism,
gay rights, and environmentalism on the left; pro-life and pro-family
movements on the right. Domestic disputes paralleled arguments over
how to respond to threats and opportunities abroad, where Cold War
anxieties, briefly revived in the 1980s, shifted after the fall of the Soviet
Union onto international networks of terror. Partisanship sharpened
as conservatives and traditionalists unified under the banner of the
Republican Party and liberals and progressives took to a Democratic
Party now largely abandoned by what had once been its most reliable
base, whites in the solid South.

Though at home, Pentecostals were hardly at ease in this contentious Zion. White Pentecostals in particular shared the deep anxieties
of the evangelicals whose ranks they had joined, and when the alarm
sounded, they rose shoulder to shoulder with their peers to defend the
endangered moral fabric and the embattled Judeo-Christian heritage
of their nation. In the process, Pentecostalism made its belated political
turn, rising from the political margins to become a major factor in U.S.
party politics.

Political engagement simultaneously revealed a narrowing gap
between Pentecostalism and parts of the American mainstream and a
widening gap within the movement itself. Even as Pentecostals acted
to heal racial divisions that had long scarred the movement, their
political turn demonstrated just how deeply those differences ran:
white Pentecostals joined white evangelicals in the Religious Right
and the Republican Party, while African American Pentecostals took
their place in the Black Church, which, since the 1960s, had become
one of the Democratic Party's most dependable constituencies. In both
cases, the new alliances were facilitated by the reciprocal evolution
of the allies. Pentecostal acculturation, that is, was matched by the
Pentecostalization of both the Black Church and white evangelicalism,
so that the mainstream currents Pentecostals now joined more closely
resembled the revised ethos and assumptions of their own movement.

The culture wars took shape against the backdrop of economic woes,
which at least partly explained the retreat from idealism and the rising
individualistic mood that followed the Sixties. The long post–World
War II expansion first stalled and then collapsed in the oil embargo and

recession of 1973, which introduced a period of stagflation followed by a series of boom-bust cycles that had coughed up four more major recessions by 2008. Downsizing and wage stagnation set the tone for U.S. workers. As New Deal and Great Society supports eroded and globalization took hold, poverty ticked upward in an increasingly service-oriented economy. Meanwhile, a smaller share of the populace corralled a larger share of the nation's total wealth, with statistical inequality edging back toward Gilded Age levels.

Yet, middle America never lost its Horatio Alger faith in the rags-to-riches story, so that economic malaise and rising individualism interacted with that unflappable optimism to set the stage for a new edition of the gospel of prosperity, one that modulated the old deliverance theme to a teaching mode more suited to the tenor of the day. Under the tutelage of a gifted generation of Pentecostal and neo-charismatic teachers, thousands of saints embraced the tantalizing belief that one's heaven-touched American dream lay only a word of faith away.

That being said, the Cold War juxtaposition of optimism and anxiety continued, with nuclear doomsday scenarios now augmented by environmental ones, inspired by catastrophes like the Santa Barbara and Exxon Valdez oil spills, toxic meltdowns at Three-Mile Island and Chernobyl, and growing alarm over the potentially devastating effect of global climate change. Together with the rise of radical Islam and the ongoing cycle of violence surrounding the state of Israel, these developments rejuvenated millenarian expectations among many Pentecostals, prompting a new emphasis on prophecy and the Second Coming. The faithful consecrated their hearts anew lest they be "left behind" in the coming Rapture.

Pentecostalism had internationalized within years of its inception. Now, that aspect of the movement heightened as globalization created greater interdependency and compressed the human geography of the world. Americans reached out to the world more easily and often, and the world more easily and often came to America. Immigration reforms effected in the 1960s, for example, opened the way to levels of immigration in the 1980s and 1990s that had not been seen since the turn of the last century. Unlike the old immigration, however, this wave was dominated by newcomers from places like Latin America and Asia who increased the racial diversity of the nation and eroded the majority status of ethnically European Americans.

These trends affected Pentecostalism in complex ways. Nonwhites had always been disproportionately represented in the movement. At the same time, Pentecostalism had flourished more luxuriantly abroad than it had in the United States, so that the vast majority of the world's Pentecostals were by this time non-American, and indeed non-Western. Now, immigration further sharpened the racial diversity of U.S. Pentecostalism. Of even greater significance, foreign-born Pentecostals increasingly imported their own versions of Pentecostalism into the movement's birthplace, with some robust foreign organizations sending "reverse missionaries" to organize congregations among immigrants from the homeland or to plant new churches in the mission fields of America.

All of these developments, to one degree or another, were shaped by the central technological revolution of the day. Where past eras had been reconfigured by shifts in fundamental modes of transportation and communication—the automobile and airplane; the telephone, radio, and television—the last quarter of the 20th century absorbed a revolution in the transmission and manipulation of data. Once again, Pentecostals displayed their instinctive technological modernism. By the first decade of the 21st century, it seemed that everywhere one turned, Web sites, podcasts, social networking sites, blogs, and streaming video dispensed Spirit and power for the digital age.

A PENTECOST OF POLITICS

The transformation of Pentecostalism over these years is perhaps best viewed through the lens of its evolving political culture. An observer once described the 1892 Populist convention as a "Pentecost of politics." Yet, Pentecostalism proper usually wanted no part of that pairing. As in the case of A. J. Tomlinson, when the Holy Ghost moved in, the "old man" moved out, and he took his secular politicking with him.

To be sure, the unruly movement fell short of uniformity on the point, as it did on many others. The record shows a smattering of local Pentecostal officials by the 1920s and 1930s, including a sheriff, a police chief, a justice of the peace, a couple of state party leaders, a mayor, and a state legislator.[1] Not surprisingly, the most notorious exception to the rule came in the person of Aimee Semple McPherson. Her earliest forays into politics lent support to largely unsuccessful efforts to legislate religious or moral standards for the greater Los Angeles area, such as ballot measures to place the Bible in public schools, prohibit the teaching of evolution, and deny Venice Beach an exemption from so-called blue laws. In addition, McPherson publicly endorsed candidates at all levels of office, including Herbert Hoover in the 1928 presidential election. A favored cause was Prohibition, and, when support for the Eighteenth Amendment began to waver, she joined forces with an old adversary who shared her Prohibitionist zeal—socialist Upton Sinclair—by hosting a much-ballyhooed 1932 debate on the issue that Sinclair moderated. (The marriage of convenience failed to last; McPherson campaigned against Sinclair and for Republican Frank Merriam when Sinclair ran for governor two years later.) McPherson, though, was a bipartisan endorser. William Jennings Bryan spoke frequently at Angelus Temple, and she gave aid and air time to candidates of any party who professed Christian values and shared her "Christian America" assumptions.[2]

Most Pentecostal leaders of McPherson's day, though, felt strongly that the church should not "leave its place in the Kingdom of God to dabble in the affairs of men." Rather than "entering into politics," Christians should win souls for Christ and live holy lives in "separation from the world."[3] The typical Pentecostal response to social dilemmas was to save souls, not cast ballots.

But if McPherson was atypical, she pointed the way to the movement's future nonetheless. Upward social mobility and integration into wider evangelicalism altered the movement's political ethos so that, by the 1950s, distinct signs of increased interest—along with conservative political leanings—had surfaced, as for example in Richard Nixon's address before the 1954 convention of the Full Gospel Business Men's Fellowship International.

These tendencies, however, remained mostly latent. A few Pentecostals entered the political arena, such as J. R. Flower, elected to the Springfield, Missouri, city council, but no large-scale turn to politics followed. That awaited the arrival of two great social challenges. The first was the civil rights movement; the second the countercultural unrest of the 1960s. Pentecostals responded to the two challenges differently, but each challenge in its own way furthered the politicization of Pentecostalism.

PENTECOSTALISM AND CIVIL RIGHTS

We have seen that the Pentecostal record on race, when viewed in the context of its times, was less deplorable than the norm. Yet the vast majority of the movement had segregated by the 1930s (a process often rationalized as a pragmatic concession to the social prejudices of others), and Pentecostals responded ambiguously to the civil rights activism that followed *Brown v. Board of Education* (1954). The Church of God (COG; Cleveland, Tennessee), which in 1926 had organized blacks into a separate branch under a white general overseer, initially opposed integration; and the Assemblies of God (AG), where de facto segregation was the norm, continued to recommend that blacks seek affiliation with the Church of God in Christ (COGIC). Many districts of the AG, in fact, had come by the 1950s to refuse to ordain African Americans. The flip-flop on race found its keenest illustration in the Northern California–Nevada district, which in 1951 declined to license evangelist Robert Harrison, even though his grandmother, Cornelia Jones Robertson, had been ordained by that very district in the 1920s.[4]

Silver linings did exist. Interracial worship still occurred, especially in smaller bodies like the Church of God of Prophecy and on the movement's fringe, as, for example, in the serpent-handling Dolly Pond Church of God. The AG and the COGIC, moreover, exchanged fraternal representatives at their annual assemblies in the mid-1950s. And quite bold voices for racial equality resounded from beneath the movement's tents. Deliverance evangelists like Oral Roberts, Jack Coe, and A. A. Allen defied racist taboos by integrating their southern campaigns, courting black support, and openly condemning segregation. And from the time Oral Roberts University opened its doors, it ranked among the top universities in the nation in the category of black enrollment at predominantly white institutions. For all that could be said against them, and notwithstanding the entrepreneurial self-interest of their actions, Pentecostal healers led the way on civil rights.

The major white Pentecostal denominations, however, equivocated or fell silent at the onset of the civil rights movement. In 1956, the AG appointed a committee on race relations that basically advised inaction. "We could not afford to go on record as favoring integration," explained General Superintendent Ralph Riggs. "Neither did we want it to be known that we were in favor of segregation." Thus, AG leaders decided to "mark time," waiting for public opinion on the matter to settle.[5] Like other white denominations, the AG chose to follow, not lead, on civil rights.

By contrast, black Pentecostals rolled up their sleeves and joined the fray, though less vigorously than did other black Protestants. This was not entirely new: black Pentecostals like William Roberts, Robert Clarence Lawson, and Arenia Mallory had labored in the civil rights trenches long before the breakthroughs of the 1950s, with Mallory serving on Eleanor Roosevelt's Negro Women's Cabinet and Lawson joining other Harlem clergy in jobs campaigns led by Adam Clayton Powell, Jr.

At the peak of the civil rights movement, then, black Pentecostals were positioned to respond. Smallwood Williams served as president of the Washington, DC, chapter of the Southern Christian

Leadership Conference and as a delegate to the Democratic National Convention. J. O. Patterson, Sr., Ithiel Clemmons, and Herbert Daughtry distinguished themselves for their efforts in Memphis and New York City. And Mallory again answered the call of duty, this time as a consultant on labor issues for the Kennedy administration. Meanwhile, individual congregations stood at the front lines of the conflict. Black Pentecostal churches were bombed by white segregationists, and Martin Luther King, Jr., delivered his final sermon at Mason Temple, the headquarters of the COGIC in Memphis, Tennessee.

Eventually, the white denominations came around. By 1959, AG missionaries in Africa were complaining that reports of racism in the United States hindered their efforts in newly independent African nations. At the same time, the broader evangelical world began to align against racism, led by its most prominent spokesperson, Billy Graham, who seemed to challenge the AG directly when he added Harrison to his crusade team. Pressure from within the denominations came from enlightened figures like John L. Meares, pastor of the interracial Washington Revival Center in Washington, DC, one of the largest congregations in the COG. Then, in the mid-1960s, a new generation of leaders took the helm and the consensus shifted. One white denomination after another declared its unqualified support for racial equality, with the AG and the COG now leading the way. Each passed resolutions affirming equality and condemning discrimination, and in 1966 the COG dissolved its separate Colored Assembly.

Over the following years, Harrison emerged as a prominent evangelist within the AG, addressing race and other social issues with the full backing of his denomination; the Pentecostal Holiness Church formalized ties with the United Holy Church as sister denominations; and the COG added the first black member to its governing Council of Twelve. The trend toward racial reconciliation culminated in 1994, when a Pentecostal Partners conference convened in Memphis, Tennessee, to address the movement's racial divide. Dubbed the Memphis Miracle, it prompted leaders to disband the all-white Pentecostal Fellowship of North America and replace it with the racially integrated Pentecostal/Charismatic Churches of North America.

Despite having taken significant strides toward racial healing, the differing responses of black and white Pentecostals to the civil rights movement revealed sharply distinct political outlooks. For white Pentecostals, increasingly self-identified as evangelical, the issue of race had largely been filtered through the prism of theology and personal ethics, not politics. For black Pentecostals, increasingly self-identified as members of the Black Church, issues of race and social justice seemed inherently political, matters for legal and social-structural remedy, not merely religious conversion or moral persuasion. Black Pentecostals remained more conservative than their non-Pentecostal allies, but the civil rights struggle left them far more supportive of Great Society–style intervention on behalf of the needy and oppressed than were their white Pentecostal kin.

THE POLITICAL TURN

For white Pentecostals, the last push into the rough and tumble of partisan politics came somewhat later and from a different source: the avalanche of wrenching transformations that rumbled across the social and cultural landscape in the 1960s and 1970s. These were disturbing times for religious conservatives. The antiwar movement challenged authority, disrupted public tranquility, and thumbed its nose at patriotism, while the counterculture pushed sexual license, drug use, political radicalism, and hedonistic forms of music, dress, and lifestyle. Meanwhile, the Supreme Court disallowed mandatory prayer and Bible reading in the public schools and loosened restrictions on obscenity. To make matters worse, the teaching of evolution became standard in the public schools, and some school districts even introduced sex education. The seismic shifts of the Sixties continued into the early 1970s, when Congress passed the Equal Rights Amendment (1972), the Supreme Court legalized abortion on demand (1973), and feminism and the gay rights movement took wing.

Americans of more liberal persuasion, of course, welcomed the sweep of post–civil rights changes as the arc of progress, a vital widening of participatory democracy, personal liberty, and social justice. But conservatives responded with outrage and alarm. Taken together, these trends introduced a new source of conservative solidarity: the conviction that an unholy alliance subsumed under the general heading of secular humanism had laid siege to Christian America, placing the spiritual and political foundations of the nation, indeed, the very fabric of society, at risk.

For many, that sense of siege fostered a new apocalyptic turn, a taut expectation of the Second Coming that lifted Hal Lindsey's *Late, Great Planet Earth* (1970) to astonishing heights of popularity. But for many others—indeed for many of the same—it shattered the last barrier to political engagement. Extraordinary times demanded extraordinary measures, they reasoned, including political ones. And because many of these disturbing currents were tied in the public mind to the Democratic Party, the politicization of fundamentalists and evangelicals played a major role in the white evangelical shift to the GOP. Indeed, 1964 marked the last time Democrats would win a majority of the white evangelical vote in a general election.

Pentecostals lagged behind their fundamentalist and evangelical peers when it came to enthusiasm for politics, but they moved in the same direction. One of the first intrusions into politics by a major Pentecostal official came in 1960, when Thomas Zimmerman publicly warned against the prospect of a Catholic president. But that warning harked back to the stock villains of a previous day, and grassroots Pentecostal discourse about Kennedy often strayed far from a truly political calculation of interests; after 1963, many parlors buzzed with speculation about the "beast" of Revelation 13, a figure of the anti-Christ who would be worshiped by all after a deadly head wound had been miraculously healed. But by the late 1960s, Pentecostal pronouncements hewed more closely to mainstream concerns. A 1968 statement from the AG, for example, denounced revolution and social protest, though it still insisted that the best thing one could do in these troubled times was preach the "gospel of the Lord Jesus Christ."[6]

If white Pentecostals stepped slowly into outright political action, they marched lockstep with other evangelicals on the issues, cheering grassroots campaigns against corrupting textbooks in West Virginia, gay rights in Florida, and ratification of the Equal Rights Amendment. Pentecostal bodies issued social statements that rejected feminism and affirmed the beleaguered traditional family, and a few Pentecostals did plunge headlong into the political waters. Timothy Johnson won a seat on the Urbana, Illinois, city council in 1971, which he parlayed into a long career in state politics and then a seat in the United States House of Representatives. The following year, in neighboring Missouri, the Yale-educated son of the president of Evangel College, John Ashcroft, ran for Congress. He lost, but was appointed Missouri state auditor and began a rise to political power that would carry him to the governor's house, the United States Senate, and the office of the U.S. attorney general. Meanwhile, Albert Robinson won a seat in the Kentucky House of Representatives, beginning decades of service as a crusader for conservative Christian values in that state's legislature.

As their political interest deepened, Pentecostals followed the evangelical lead beyond longstanding fixations on quasi-political issues like evolution and the sexual dictates of so-called pelvic theology into sympathy with a broader agenda of conventional political concerns, including the new GOP critique of big government. On the one hand, the ideal of limited government meshed well with the apolitical instincts of Pentecostals and other sectarians, who had always looked to churches, private charity, and personal initiative for solutions to social problems. Now, that ideal sharpened as Supreme Court decisions, congressional legislation, and Internal Revenue Service scrutiny of the tax-exempt status of private religious schools convinced many that government itself posed a threat to religion and morality. On the other hand, this shift revealed the movement's susceptibility to an old-fashioned populist (small *p*) sleight of hand tracing back as far as Davy Crockett's *Advice to Politicians:* the tactic of rousing the irascible masses by denouncing government as a means of winning election to it. Governing with an antigovernment aspect has always been paradoxically combined, of course, with jingoistic demands for patriotic loyalty— "my country right or wrong"—relative to those governmental actions one supports.

Be that as it may, Pentecostals and other religious conservatives soon gathered around a political consensus that was profamily, proreligion, probusiness, prodefense, anticommunist, and anti–big government (with the notable exceptions of law enforcement and defense, where government could hardly be big enough). They sought to enlist government in the maintenance of public order and morality but limit its interference in religion and the economy.

Strong sentiments and shared opinions, however, do not automatically translate into meaningful political action. That requires structure and organization. The turning point here came in the mid-1970s, when political matchmakers like Ed McAteer of the Religious Roundtable; Richard Viguerie, publisher of *Conservative Digest;* and Paul Weyrich of the Committee for the Survival of a Free Congress brought New Right conservatives and evangelical leaders into a lasting union known as the Religious Right. They did not start from scratch. Wealthy industrialists like J. Howard Pew (Sun Oil), Richard DeVos (Amway), and Joseph Coors, together with evangelicals like Bill Bright, had diligently courted pietistic Christians since the 1950s. But now, the time was ripe as never before. A network of politically oriented ministries and organizations sprang up—the National Christian Action Coalition, Jerry Falwell's Moral Majority, James Dobson's Focus on the Family, Robert Grant's Christian Voice, Lou Sheldon's Traditional Values Coalition, and Weyrich's Heritage Foundation—that brought religious conservatives of many types, including Pentecostals, into a potent and explicitly political alliance.

Meanwhile, televangelists who had risen from the fertile intersection of the Pentecostal, charismatic, and evangelical worlds did their part to steer Pentecostals into the political turn. Pat Robertson's

Christian Broadcasting Network and offshoots like Paul Crouch's Trinity Broadcasting Network (TBN) and Jim Bakker's *PTL Club* blended Pentecostal spirituality with political analysis, all in a high-toned studio atmosphere that appealed to the audience's upward social aspirations. Robertson's *700 Club,* in particular, evolved into a political education seminar, brimming with commentary and urgent calls to action. And by the end of the 1970s, Jimmy Swaggart had risen to prominence. Though a master of old-fashioned Pentecostal preaching who criticized rivals for their worldly concerns, Swaggart proved second to none in his frank advocacy of political causes.

The rise of private Christian academies as an alternative to the public school system also played a role. When Pentecostals ventured into elementary and secondary education, they joined Christian school and home schooling movements that had historically embraced a Christian America outlook, mediated through both informal norms and standard curriculum on "Christian Americanism." Furthermore, such ventures formed part and parcel of a heightened emphasis on education within an increasingly middle-class movement. Here as elsewhere, rising educational attainment—particularly when it occurred within the evangelical or Pentecostal subcultures—correlated with greater political involvement and greater attachment to the canons of conservative politics.

Although the born-again Jimmy Carter piqued evangelicals' interest, he did little to mobilize them and left them feeling betrayed. The first to fully seize the potential of the Religious Right was Ronald Reagan, who truly galvanized the new movement. In addition to evangelicals, Reagan let Pentecostals and charismatics taste political success by recruiting them into his administration. There, Pentecostal Interior Secretary James Watt joined charismatics like Oral Roberts University alumna Andrea Sheldon Lafferty (daughter of Lou Sheldon and his successor at the Traditional Values Coalition) and Carolyn Sundseth, Reagan's director of public liaison, as symbols of political awakening among Spirit-filled Christians. "If Jesus Christ is going to be your Lord in every area of your life," Sundseth explained, "He has to be the Lord of your politics, too." For her and many others, the Lordship of Christ and the presidency of Ronald Reagan went hand in hand.

With Reagan as a fitting object of their deepening political inclinations, the 1980s witnessed a surge of political action and rhetoric in Pentecostal circles. John Gimenez, Pentecostal pastor of Rock Church in Virginia Beach, Virginia, organized a Washington for Jesus Rally in April 1980 that drew an estimated crowd of 200,000 to the nation's capital. The rally's leaders, including cochairs Pat Robertson and

Bill Bright, refused to make an endorsement, but their opposition to homosexuality and abortion and their resounding support for prayer in the public schools made it clear that Reagan's Republicans were the party of choice.

Pentecostal and charismatic publications like *Logos Journal, Charisma, New Wine,* and *The Forerunner* likewise rang with political themes, while pastors increasingly urged churchgoers to register and vote. "I have had to repent and ask God to forgive me about not engaging in political activities," one AG pastor confided. "Twenty or thirty years ago we expected Jesus to come any time—so why get involved in changing the world?" But he had had a change of heart. "People have to vote," he explained, "and they should know what they are voting for."[7]

As America's culture wars escalated, the historic pattern of episodic conservative-liberal disputes expanded into a comprehensive social divide that cut across religious communities as much as it cut between them. Sociologist Robert Wuthnow called it the *Restructuring of American Religion* (1988). The gravitational pull drawing Pentecostals into the right wing of that divide strengthened, and with new organizations like the Family Research Council, Concerned Women of America, the Christian Coalition, and the Freedom Council augmenting the existing panoply of advocacy and interest groups in the Religious Right, value conservatism appeared to be synonymous with political action in general, and political action through the agency of the Republican Party in particular. Pentecostals had become full-fledged members of the Religious Right, fired by core issues, mobilized by savvy organizers, and activated through institutions strong enough to bring them into common cause with conservatives in the very body Zimmerman had once warned against: the Roman Catholic Church.

Against this backdrop, another wave of Pentecostal politicians rose from the ranks. At the state and local level, figures like Veo Easley, Arkansas state legislator, and Keith Butler, Detroit city council member, found their way into office; on the national scene, Pat Robertson vied for the 1988 Republican presidential nomination. Robertson, a charismatic Christian, drew strong support from classical Pentecostals, and though his bid to inherit Reagan's mantle fell short, he placed second in three of the first four primaries and finished the race ranked third in the popular vote. On the other side of the political aisle, another colorful and controversial figure, Al Sharpton, rose to prominence. Meanwhile, a vivacious young athlete, musician, and beauty pageant queen reared in the Wasilla Assembly of God had finished college and returned to her Alaska home. Soon, Sarah Palin would turn her thoughts to the local political scene.

During the 1990s, Pentecostals reaped the harvest of the previous decade's political labor. Four Pentecostals took seats in the House of Representatives—Jo Ann Davis (R, Virginia), Rick Hill (R, Montana); Marilyn Musgrave (R, Colorado); and Todd Tiahrt (R, Kansas)—while John Ensign (R, Nevada) won election to the U.S. Senate. At the state and local levels, Marylin Linfoot Shannon joined the Oregon state senate, while Bill Hardiman won the Kentwood, Michigan, mayoral race. Among African Americans, Leah Daughtry, daughter of pastor and civil rights activist Herbert Daughtry, joined the Clinton-Gore transition team and served with distinction in the Department of Labor. And in 1992 Sarah Palin launched her meteoric career with a seat on the Wasilla city council. Four years later, she was the town's mayor.

Pentecostals continued to expand their influence and office holding into the new century, where in 2006 Palin became the youngest person and only woman to be elected governor of Alaska. Then, the 2008 presidential race brought Pentecostals into the political limelight as never before. Megachurch televangelists like John Hagee of Cornerstone Church in San Antonio, Texas, and Rod Parsley of World Harvest Church in Akron, Ohio, drew fire for their controversial endorsements of John McCain, who then shocked critics and supporters alike by naming Sarah Palin as his running mate.

Palin, for her part, vaulted onto the national stage, a Rorschach test in updo, prompting cheers, mockery, dismay, or befuddlement according to the ideological makeup of the viewer. She drew raucous crowds and frenzied media wherever she went, leaving McCain to sulk in the shadow of her "rogue" celebrity. The last echo of his concession speech had scarcely cleared the air when Palin 2012 T-shirts went on sale at christianshirts.net.

Among Democrats, Daughtry—already chief of staff to Democratic National Committee chair Howard Dean—was named chief executive officer of the Democratic National Convention Committee. And following his election, Barack Obama, who had courted evangelicals and other religious voters throughout his campaign in a frantic effort to close the "God gap," chose Pentecostal minister Joshua DuBois to head his White House Office of Faith-Based and Neighborhood Partnerships.

PENTECOSTAL POLITICAL CULTURE

Under the glow of campaign lights and the scrutiny of social surveys, a portrait of Pentecostal political culture in the 21st century has emerged. Three things are clear. First, Pentecostals are active in politics with their opinions, their votes, and as candidates for public office. They still register to vote in somewhat smaller numbers than do other evangelicals, but their rate of registration is high—near 80 percent—and their involvement finds support at the highest denominational levels. In a 2004 interview, Thomas Trask, then general superintendent of the AG, declared that "believers must exercise their God-given...responsibility to vote."[8] Second, Pentecostals are sharply divided by race, with a majority of black Pentecostals supporting the progressive goals of the Democratic Party, while white Pentecostals fall overwhelmingly on the conservative side of the fence. Finally, extraordinary growth has turned Pentecostalism into a coveted political prize.

Viewed as a group, Pentecostals are more traditional in their religious and social views, more ethnically diverse, younger, more female, and less highly educated than the national norm. They continue to fall somewhat lower on the socioeconomic scale. They are more likely than the average American to say that religious groups should express their views on political issues, that political leaders should have strong religious beliefs, and that God fulfills God's purposes through politics and elections. In one recent survey, 54 percent self-identified as conservative, the second-highest ranking among all denominational families surveyed. Most of the rest identified themselves as moderate. Pentecostal liberals exist, but they are few and far between. When asked by surveyors if government "should make our country more Christian" or if we "should have separation of church and state," 52 percent of Pentecostals chose the former. Only 25 percent of the general public would agree. And though 66 percent supported a robust defense of free speech, that number fell well short of the 82 percent of the general public holding that view.[9]

Exceptions can certainly be found to this rather reactionary profile, and not only among African American Pentecostals. For example, ethicists Eldin Villafañe and Murray Dempster, social historian Augustus Cerillo, Jr., and biblical scholar Russell Spittler carry forward a countercurrent dating back at least as far as the 1970s, when the progressive opinion journal, *Agora*, began its short and rocky tenure (1977–1981). More recently, AG pastor and theologian Paul Alexander and others have founded Pentecostals and Charismatics for Peace and Justice, which publishes *Pax Pneuma*. Notwithstanding these exceptions, the data make clear that, for white Pentecostals at least, political engagement now occurs overwhelmingly under the rubric of the Religious Right and to the benefit of the Republican Party. And even among black Pentecostals, support for the Democratic Party, though strong, falls well short of that found among other black Christians.[10]

Throughout the journey to political engagement recounted above, a rising chorus of civil religion bore the leitmotiv to the movement's politicization. Civil religion is best thought of not as a separate entity—a kind of adjunct to one's religious tradition—but rather as the process whereby a tradition, drawing on its own premises and sources, sacralizes the nation and its purposes, incorporating an idealized understanding of them along with certain civic rituals and symbols into the framework of its own distinctive piety. By the early 21st century, millions of Pentecostals had in just this way gathered America under the shelter of their sacred canopy, attributing to it an essentially evangelical Christian past, a sacred nature, and a prophetic destiny wherein the United States played an instrumental role, alongside Israel, in God's End Time plan for the world. This in itself was something of a miracle: the merger of dispensationalism with manifest destiny.

THE WIDE, WIDE WORLD

As the movement's political conversion illustrates, the final decades of the 20th century saw much of Pentecostalism open itself, tentatively at least, to cooperation beyond the limits of the National Association of Evangelicals. In 1972, for example, Pentecostalism's apostle to the ecumenical world, David du Plessis, recruited kindred spirits like Spittler and historian Mel Robeck, both of the AG, and historian and church executive Vinson Synan of the Pentecostal Holiness Church into a Pentecostal–Roman Catholic dialogue that continued for a full decade. Slowly but surely, even du Plessis's detractors began to come around. Old-line distrust of charismatics thawed. A new generation of Pentecostals—better educated, more irenic, more eager to engage the world—moved into positions of leadership and migrated toward the common ground that du Plessis had surveyed. By the 1980s, du Plessis had come full circle. Now celebrated as the grand old man of moderate Pentecostalism, the AG welcomed him back and reinstated his credentials.

In some cases, Pentecostal and charismatic overlap seemed to force cooperation between the movements' leaders. When Christian Growth Ministries with its shepherding or discipleship emphasis emerged in the mid-1970s, controversy swirled around its teaching that every Christian should submit to "the 'covering' authority of a 'spiritual leader.'"[11] Alarmed by the rapid spread of the teaching through Pentecostal and charismatic circles and fearing its potential for authoritarian abuse, a concert of notables rose up against it, including Demos Shakarian,

Kathryn Kuhlman, Pat Robertson, Dennis Bennett, and Larry Christensen. A series of consultations called the Glencoe meetings convened to address the controversy.

Those consultations, in turn, impressed leaders with the need to bring classical Pentecostals, Protestant charismatics, and Catholic charismatics—the "three streams" of renewal—together in a more formal way. Their vision came to fruition in the 1977 Kansas City Conference on Charismatic Renewal in the Churches. Guided by an executive committee representing each of the three streams, the conference drew 50,000 registered attendees, including major figures like papal liaison Leon-Joseph Cardinal Suenens and J. O. Patterson and Thomas Zimmerman, heads of the COGIC and AG, respectively.

Mass gatherings of this kind quickly became a fixture on the Pentecostal-charismatic landscape, and though none quite reached the heights of Kansas City, they bore witness to an unprecedented level of unity across the Spirit-filled spectrum. "Jesus '78," organized by Dan Malachuk and Father Jim Ferry, brought 50,000 to Meadowlands, New Jersey. In 1982, the AG hosted a Conference on the Holy Spirit in Springfield, Missouri, where Dennis Bennett was fêted and Zimmerman explicitly endorsed the charismatic movement. Four years later, a leadership conference, the North American Congress on the Holy Spirit and World Evangelization, convened in New Orleans. With Synan chairing a broadly representative steering committee, Pentecostal denominations participated in greater numbers than ever before. A second, public congress held in New Orleans the following year drew a crowd of 40,000 along with celebrity speakers from across the charismatic and Pentecostal worlds. Similar events continued to attract large crowds and to inspire shared identity among Spirit-filled Christians into the 21st century, with conferences at Indianapolis in 1990, Orlando in 1995, St. Louis in 2000, and the 2001 Pentecostal World Conference in Los Angeles leading the way.

CONVERGENCE

Denominations provided the motive force of Pentecostalism during most of its first century, but by the end of the 20th century the center of dynamism had begun to shift to the zones where denominational Pentecostalism, independent Pentecostalism, and the charismatic movement converged and overlapped. As barriers dropped between these spheres, subtle changes in self-understanding took hold among many Spirit-filled believers. Where researchers once met fairly high walls between Pentecostals and charismatics, with respondents choosing one or the other self-ascription but not both, a greater willingness to blur the boundaries had emerged by the 21st century.[12]

In some cases, classical Pentecostals steered toward charismatic waters, as with the International Church of the Foursquare Gospel, where Jack Hayford—Foursquare president from 2004 to 2009 and founding pastor of the 10,000-member Church on the Way in Van Nuys, California—rose to become a leading figure in the charismatic movement. Conversely, charismatic institutions like Robertson's Regent University came to rely heavily on students and distinguished faculty from classical Pentecostal backgrounds. The ease of border crossing increased yet further with the so-called third wave of renewal, a post-1980s enlivening of traditional evangelical churches characterized by openness to spiritual gifts, but without the adoption of doctrinaire positions about them.

Independents and start-ups were especially well positioned to seize opportunities in a religious marketplace now shaped by generation X and generation Y consumers, who ranked quality, content, and personalized services above denominational labels. Church leaders, to be sure, continued to promote brand loyalty, but in a religious climate molded by the therapeutic demands of consumer-oriented "seekers," the rank-and-file was inclined to drink from refreshing streams wherever it might find them. The value of denominational structures became an increasingly hard sell.

These factors opened the way for dramatic growth within unconventional and often youth-oriented networks of churches that resisted categorization as full-fledged denominations and skirted the margins of Pentecostal-charismatic identity. For example, Maranatha Christian Churches, a Jesus Movement offshoot founded in the early 1970s by Jewish convert and former AG youth pastor Bob Weiner, had expanded into a federation of scores of congregations in more than a dozen nations by 1989, when Weiner's resignation effectively disbanded the organization. A more enduring example is the Calvary Chapel movement, where Chuck Smith's Southern California congregation had by 2010 mushroomed into a fellowship of more than 1,400 churches and a half-million adherents worldwide. But the Vineyard provides the best illustration of Pentecostal, charismatic, and evangelical convergence.

The Vineyard movement began in the mid-1970s with a church by that name affiliated with Smith's Calvary Chapel. Founded by Kenn Gulliksen, the first Vineyard met in the home of Christian rock pioneer Chuck Girard and was noted for its free-wheeling manifestations of the Holy Spirit. The congregation flourished, and Gulliksen planted several other Vineyards over the next few years. Meanwhile, a congregation led by church growth expert John Wimber had also affiliated with Calvary Chapel.

It soon became apparent that a difference of emphasis existed between the more overtly charismatic churches associated with Gulliksen, Wimber, and Lonnie Frisbee and the relatively sedate model preferred by Smith. In 1983, by mutual agreement, the more demonstrative group separated under the Vineyard name, with Wimber at the helm. From that point forward, the Association of Vineyard Churches rivaled or even exceeded Calvary Chapel in its rate of expansion. By 2010, it claimed over 550 churches in the United States and 1,500 worldwide.[13]

At first, Vineyard displayed little direct classical Pentecostal influence. Its effervescent style derived more from Gulliksen and the pragmatic orientation of Wimber, whose research had confirmed a link between signs and wonders and church growth. But as the movement spread, it drew Pentecostal congregations and individuals into its fold. By 2010, 3 of the 10 members of its governing board—including national director Bert Waggoner—had come to Vineyard by way of classical Pentecostal backgrounds. Finally, as Vineyard's identity evolved, it staked its claim at the intersection of the renewal movements, where "empowered evangelicals" combined "the best of the evangelical and charismatic worlds."[14]

In many respects, Waggoner himself has personified convergence. The son of a pastor and district superintendent in the Pentecostal Church of God (PCG), Waggoner graduated from the denomination's Southern Bible College in Houston, Texas, in the 1960s and later returned to chair its Department of Bible and Theology. In 1976, he left the classroom to plant an inner-city congregation, Church of the Redeemed, under the auspices of the PCG. Then, Waggoner's relationship with his old denomination soured.

Within classical Pentecostalism, differences among denominations are often less theological than cultural, deriving from subtle variations in the prevailing norms of dress, music, rhetoric, and worship that set the parameters of authentic experience for the group. Waggoner's youth-oriented, urban congregation did not fit easily within PCG parameters. His relaxed approach to sartorial taboos and his congregation's "charismatic" style of worship—including a preference for praise choruses over traditional Pentecostal hymns—ruffled the feathers of traditionalists in the denomination.

Rather than stay and fight, Waggoner transferred his affiliation to the more open-minded AG, merging Church of the Redeemed with a nearby Assemblies congregation, Church in the City. In the mid-1980s,

Waggoner led Church in the City into the Association of Vineyard Churches, although he continued to hold credentials with the AG until 1989. Waggoner later founded a thriving Vineyard congregation in Sugarland, Texas, and served as a Vineyard regional director until his 2000 appointment to succeed Todd Hunter as the denomination's national director.[15]

One of the major contributions of the Vineyard and other like groups has been the promotion of a theological framework, called kingdom theology, capable of sustaining fellowship across the evangelical-charismatic-Pentecostal continuum. Viewed as an alternative to dispensationalism, which in their view fixates on eschatology and narrows the divine drama to two main characters (Israel and the Church), kingdom theology places greater emphasis on the redemptive role of the believer in society and thus reunites social ethics and personal morality.

African American circles were deeply influenced by similar forms of convergence. Although the neo-Pentecostalization of black Protestantism took place a decade or so after the charismatic renewal of the predominately white mainline churches, it proved to be, if anything, more thorough. By the end of the 20th century, some of the largest congregations in the historic black denominations resounded with Spirit-filled worship, including St. Paul African Methodist Episcopal Church in Cambridge, Massachusetts; Allen Temple in Queens; Pilgrim Baptist Cathedral in Brooklyn; Greater St. Stephen Full Gospel Baptist Church in New Orleans; and Full Gospel African Methodist Episcopal Zion church in Temple Hills, Maryland (prior to its reorganization as the independent From the Heart Church Ministries). Indeed, one study from the mid-1990s found that 19 percent of black Protestants in non-Pentecostal bodies had spoken in tongues.[16]

Perhaps the leading example of Vineyard-style convergence in the Black Church is the Full Gospel Baptist Church Fellowship (FGBCF), founded in 1994 by Bishop Paul S. Morton, Sr., copastor of Greater St. Stephen's. Embracing "the scope of the Pentecostal movement for its spirituality, the Baptist Church for its structure, and the Word Church for its emphasis on the Word of God," the FGBCF had mushroomed into an association of several hundred congregations within 15 years of its founding.[17]

The neo-Pentecostalization of the Black Church gained impetus from the success of ministers like Thomas D. Jakes, who became the best-known and most influential minister of Oneness background since William Branham. Born in South Charleston, West Virginia, in 1957, the former Baptist converted to Oneness Pentecostalism in a small storefront church and affiliated with the Greater Emmanuel

Apostolic Faith Churches. By the age of 30, he had risen to the rank of bishop. In the early 1990s, Jakes developed a ministry to abused women around the theme "Woman, Thou Art Loosed," which became the basis for a best-selling book by that name and opened the door to weekly television programs on Trinity Broadcasting Network and Black Entertainment Television. By then Jakes was an up-and-coming celebrity. He switched his affiliation to the Higher Ground Always Abounding Assemblies and in 1996 moved to Dallas, where he founded The Potter's House, an independent, multiracial congregation that in a decade's time soared to 30,000 members. Building on his talents as a speaker, musician, and prolific writer, Jakes transformed his Dallas base into the center of a multimedia empire and soon ranked among the most powerful religious figures in the United States.

By the early 21st century, megachurches like The Potter's House had become a signature of modern Pentecostalism. Clearly, not all mega-churches were Pentecostal or charismatic, as attested by Bill Hybel's Willow Creek Church near Chicago and Rick Warren's Saddleback Church in Orange County, California. But Pentecostal and charismatic churches were disproportionately counted among the super-large. This was especially true on the global scene, where the 20 largest congregations in the world were all Pentecostal or charismatic, beginning with David Yonggi Cho's 800,000-member Yoido Full Gospel Church of Seoul, Korea, affiliated with the AG. In the United States, the list of Pentecostal megachurches had by the 21st century grown far too long to recite, but—in addition to those already mentioned—the number included Victory Christian Center in Tulsa; First Assembly of God in Phoenix; West Angeles Church of God in Christ and Crenshaw Christian Center, both in Los Angeles; Cathedral of Praise in Oklahoma City; and Calvary Temple in Irving, Texas.

Today, the megachurch stands as an important zone of convergence in its own right, both for the natural influence groups of that size exert on others and because so many share what could be called a common religious ecosphere. Most feature consumer-oriented messaging and programming, and virtually all convey an aura of success and sophistication, a thrilling sense of being where the action is that rises naturally from the scale and design of the facilities and from their conspicuous display of modern technology: open sight lines to jumbo screens dropped from steel rigging; professional-quality music filtered through high-tech mixing boards; and video cameras mounted on sweeping booms that search stage and audience for angles to broadcast via streaming Web cast or live television or for later editing into downloadable video podcasts.

But the true genius of the contemporary megachurch—apart from sheer economy of scale—rests in its knack for combining the social excitement of a mass meeting with the intimacy of a small group. The main worship service typically forms but the centerpiece of a small galaxy of activities, social services, outreach programs, special interest groups, and cozy midweek gatherings tailored to satisfy the personal tastes and individualized needs of almost everyone. That being said, the ecosphere leaves ample room for variety, with differences often symbolized in church architecture, which runs from the "un-church" style—evoking a local community center, school gymnasium, or warehouse complex—to daunting edifices like North Little Rock Pentecostal Church, with its opulent dome, 193-foot steeple, and Roman columns worthy of any Southern cathedral.

Zones of convergence like those described above have provided fertile ground for currents of revitalization, some resembling past outpourings like the New Order of the Latter Rain or even Azusa Street itself. In 1994, for example, a tide of old-fashioned revival swept the upscale Toronto Airport Vineyard. Dubbed the Toronto Blessing, it brought outbursts of glossolalia, weeping, jerking, shaking, being slain in the spirit, and a phenomenon that became the revival's trademark, "holy laughter." Those so blessed saw Azusa Street parallels in their nonstop meetings, and ecstatic manifestations, and in the missionary zeal that carried Toronto to the world and brought the world—in the form of a reported two million visitors—to Toronto.

As at Azusa Street, the press had a field day. With dozens of men and women strewn about the carpet, wrote Kenneth Woodward, "the huge new church looked like a field hospital." Leslie Scrivener of the *Toronto Star* compared it to Hurricane Opal. But "at least with Opal," she quipped, "they could stay on their feet."[18] And as at Azusa Street, the peculiar antics drew harsh fire from even the near and dear. Wimber himself disapproved. Seeing perhaps not enough sign and too much wonder, he had Toronto expelled from the Vineyard. Wimber's actions, though, had little effect. The revival had by then birthed its own supporting network of churches, pilgrims, and enthusiasts—enough collective fuel to keep the fires burning for another full decade.

Toronto, however, did not exist in isolation. It was a product of convergence, with Toronto only the central node of a much larger nexus. Pastor John Arnott and his wife Carol had experienced similar phenomena at a revival in Argentina, and fellow Vineyard pastor Randy Clark, whose meetings sparked the Toronto Blessing, had himself succumbed to holy laughter at a camp meeting led by South African Pentecostal Rodney Howard-Browne. In 1993 Howard-Browne had conducted a revival at Carpenter's Home Assemblies of God in Lakeland, Florida, with effects virtually identical to those at Toronto. Finally, in 1995, a similar but less controversial downpour fell on the Brownsville Assemblies of God in Pensacola, where evangelist Steve Hill and other leaders oversaw a spectacular revival that, like the Toronto Blessing, endured for more than a decade. By the end of the 20th century, the Pentecostal-charismatic world had become so densely interwoven that when one group shouted, others caught a blessing.

As globalization and immigration reshaped the United States, these zones of convergence became increasingly multicultural and indeed international. Reverse missions, for example, sharply increased, with Pentecostal bodies headquartered abroad founding congregations in the United States, usually by organizing immigrants from the home country but sometimes through traditional missionary outreach, with the United States as their mission field. By 2010, the chief foreign Pentecostal denominations active in the United States included the Universal Church of the Reign of God and Brazil for Christ Apostolic Church, both of Brazil; the Chinese Full Gospel Fellowship, International; Christ Apostolic Church (Nigeria); the Filipino Assemblies of the Firstborn; the First Church of Jesus Christ Apostolic (Haiti); and the Indian Pentecostal Church of God. The precondition for this phenomenon, of course, rose from the prior globalization of Pentecostalism, whose membership is now overwhelmingly concentrated outside of the United States and indeed outside of the developed world.[19]

TELEVANGELISM AND THE GOSPEL OF PROSPERITY

Over the last quarter of the 20th century, the nature of media changed. Old media bravely adapted to a world of first video- and cassette tapes, then CDs and DVDs, and finally Web sites, podcasts, blogs, Tweets, YouTube, and Facebook. Yet for all of these changes, the marriage of media and Pentecostal spirituality continued to flourish. Television, though affected, clung to its privileged place, and as a result televangelism remained the cornerstone of Pentecostal media and the premise of the movement's most visible leaders. Though rocked by scandal in the 1980s, it entered the 21st century still strong, holding its own amid the new media of the digital age.

By the early 1980s, the leading televangelists of classical Pentecostal background were Oral Roberts, the pioneering giant of televangelism, and two newcomers, Jim Bakker and Jimmy Swaggart. Never one to rest on his laurels, Roberts followed up his transition from deliverance evangelist to university founder and media titan by launching the City of Faith Medical and Research Center in 1981. The venture proved ill-advised, as demand never matched the scale of Roberts's overbuilt enterprise, which boasted 30-story and 20-story facilities adjacent to a 60-story medical center—one of the tallest buildings in the state. Despite desperate fundraising efforts, the City of Faith folded after a short decade of operation. But Roberts's university and his media conglomerate survived. In the late 1990s, Roberts passed the mantle to his son, Richard, who took charge of the Oral Roberts Evangelistic Association and produced a weekly television program that was still being broadcast on more than 200 stations worldwide at the time of the elder Roberts's death in December 2009.

The boyish Jim Bakker, a native of Muskegon Heights, Michigan, and graduate of the AG's North Central Bible College, rose to fame as a protégé of Pat Robertson, hosting a children's program on the Christian Broadcasting Network, where he soon became a *700 Club* fixture. The effusive Bakker possessed uncanny talents as a fundraiser, and quickly emerged as the star of the network's fundraising telethons. In addition, he promoted the *700 Club*'s fortuitous shift to a call-in talk show format, where the best attributes of the telethon were merged with those of a Johnny Carson–style late-night talk show. As a frequent host of his brainchild program, Bakker's popularity soared.

Buoyed by his new fame, Bakker broke with Robertson and teamed with fellow AG member Paul Crouch to found Trinity Broadcasting Network. But in 1974, Bakker abandoned the fledgling network to launch his own program, the *PTL Club* ("Praise the Lord" or "People that Love") in Charlotte, North Carolina. Bakker's start-up proved to be an enormous success, and by the mid-1980s PTL had expanded into a $170 million concern headquartered at the lavish Heritage U.S.A., a Fort Mill, South Carolina, retreat center, television studio, and Christian theme park.

As Bakker climbed the ladder of televangelism success, a rival surfaced who, stylistically at least, hewed more closely to the old-time Pentecostal line. The Louisiana-born Jimmy Lee Swaggart rose through the ranks of the AG as an evangelist of prodigious skill, aided by his notable talent as a singer and musician. His bluesy, rockabilly gospel style thrilled audiences and helped lift him to prominence, especially after cousin Jerry Lee Lewis convinced Sun Records to offer him a record contract. In 1969 Swaggart launched a radio program, "The Campmeeting Hour," and, as his popularity swelled, he moved from congregational meetings to citywide crusades. His first television program aired in 1973, and a decade later it reigned as the number-one syndicated religious program in the United States.

At his peak, Swaggart appeared on over 3,000 stations in 145 nations around the world, and the Jimmy Swaggart Evangelistic Association gathered annual receipts in excess of $180 million. The sprawling ministry that radiated from his 10,000-member Family Worship Center in Baton Rouge included Jimmy Swaggart Bible College, *The Evangelist* magazine, a children's relief program, and an outreach program that lent support to 600 missionaries in 117 countries. In addition, Swaggart oiled the machine of denominational fraternity by contributing millions each year to the AG.[20]

By 1987, Bakker symbolized Pentecostal success in the modern, pan-charismatic style, while Swaggart carried the banner for "orthodox" Pentecostal doctrine and the old rhetoric of confrontation (including public denunciations of country club Christians like Bakker). Scandals, though, soon swept both from their vaunted positions and dealt a heavy blow to the entire field of televangelism.

In early 1987, Tammy Fay Bakker checked into a drug rehabilitation clinic amid a cloud of rumor and innuendo. Shortly thereafter, Jim Bakker resigned from PTL Enterprises, handing the reins to Jerry Falwell and accusing enemies of attempting to blackmail him over a 1980 tryst with church secretary Jessica Hahn. The smoldering feud between Swaggart and Bakker now erupted into the open, with Swaggart cursing Bakker as "a cancer that should be excised from the body of Christ."[21] While the AG pulled Bakker's credentials, the scandal took a turn for the worse. Auditors discovered that PTL had sunk deeply into debt even as Bakker raked in millions in personal income. More damning still, Bakker appeared to have committed outright fraud by vastly overselling timeshares or "partnerships" at Heritage U.S.A. Two years later, Bakker was convicted and sent to prison, where he remained until 1994.

Swaggart, for his part, had little time to gloat over his rival's demise. The jolt of the Bakker revelations had scarcely subsided when, in early 1988, Swaggart's liaisons at seedy hotels with a local prostitute came to light. Denial was not an option, so the hell-fire evangelist confronted his transgression head-on in one of the iconic moments of 1980s television. With tears streaming down his cheeks, Swaggart stood before a packed Family Worship Center crowd and breathless viewers around the world to confess, "I have sinned." Though willing to confess his sin, Swaggart was not willing to submit to the AG's terms of discipline, and so, like Bakker, he was stripped of his credentials.

Fallout from the twin tremors touched many, but the AG was especially hard hit. By the time the dust settled, Marvin Gorman of New Orleans, David Crabtree of Des Moines, and Richard Dortch, Bakker's PTL co-conspirator, had all fallen from grace and from the AG roster. For Bakker and Swaggart, the scandals devastated but did not entirely destroy their ministries. Swaggart almost immediately began to salvage what he could of his shattered empire and, by the late 1990s, had recovered a modest but viable international ministry. After his parole, Bakker also made a minor comeback as a much-chastened and more orthodox author and teacher. The leading beneficiary of these scandals, though, proved to be Bakker's old partner, Paul Crouch, whose TBN scooped up the other networks' losses.

During the early 1990s, televangelism rebounded, though it had not seen the last of scandal. The unctuous Robert Tilton and soft-spoken Benny Hinn surged to the fore on the strength of TBN patronage, their bouffant coiffures prompting quips that televangelism, like heavy metal, had entered its "hair" phase. Tilton faltered after an ABC exposé showed that prayer requests sent to his ministry were delivered of their contributions and promptly dispatched to an open dumpster. But an old tent-meeting warrior, Robert Schambach, found a second wind as another of Crouch's favorites.

As the 21st century dawned, new celebrities like John Hagee, T. D. Jakes, Kenneth Copeland, Fred Price, Marilyn Hickey, Creflo Dollar, and Joyce Meyer crowded the stage. Along the fringes, fallen saints like Tilton and Peter Popoff—recovering from the revelation that his "words of knowledge" came by way of a hidden earphone—found a measure of grace in venues like the inspirational programming block on Black Entertainment Television. And straddling the Christian broadcasting world like a colossus was TBN, 5,000 stations and 33 satellites strong worldwide, spinning an array of programming for all ages around its flagship *Praise the Lord* variety show, including original films like *The Omega Code* and *Megiddo: The Omega Code 2* that tapped the same vein of eternally renewing Adventist expectation that had carried Tim LaHaye and Jerry Jenkins's *Left Behind* series to the top of the best-seller charts.

Today, televangelism remains strong, but it faces serious challenges. FCC deregulation has allowed paid infomercials to fill time slots once dominated by religious programming. Meanwhile, new media and media fragmentation have transformed the media environment. Low-cost production technology and local programming have expanded the options for aspiring broadcasters, as has the relative ease of do-it-yourself televangelism, where evangelists and local congregations may post their own productions on video sharing sites in hopes of going "viral" in cyberspace. Similarly, more Pentecostals now find their religious news and inspiration from blogs, Twitter, social networks, or other virtual communities.

Old Pentecostal media have struggled gamely to keep up. Magazines, radio stations, and television networks now build their own glossy Web sites to make content available online, offer video and audio downloads, interact with patrons, solicit contributions, and provide links to helpful resources or affiliated sites of interest. In that respect, the boundary between forms of media has blurred, with modern networks and ministries supplying content in almost every conceivable form.

POSITIVE CONFESSION: WEALTH
AND THE WORD OF FAITH

We have seen how televangelists like Oral Roberts adjusted to changing times by subtly altering their message as well as their technology. As the Sixties gave way to the more private and material concerns of what Thomas Wolfe dubbed the Me Decade, televangelists put their own spin on the maxim, "nothing succeeds like success," and prosperity-oriented programming came to dominate the religious airwaves. The theme seemed to touch a deep social need among Pentecostals, both as an antidote to the lean mood of stagflationary times and as a kind of collective therapy for the social stigma and economic hardship that had weighed on many of them so heavily and for so long. The ostentatious sets, technological flair, and glamorous attire featured on shows like the *PTL Club* offered vicarious vindication, proof positive that Pentecostals had arrived, that they need not take a back seat to anyone. In important ways, they changed Pentecostals' image of themselves and of their social possibilities.

Televangelism's paean to the marriage of godliness and the good life formed a natural conduit for conservative ideology. But it also made televangelism a natural fit for a potent new movement that would sweep the Pentecostal and charismatic worlds in the last decades of the 20th century. Virtually all of the old deliverance evangelists had preached the power of faith to yield financial rewards, the most famous such formula being Roberts's doctrine of Seed Faith. But by the 1970s, something had reached the stage that differed from prosperity-oriented deliverance evangelism in focus, style, and to some degree content. Rather than the charismatic deliverer exercising a spiritual gift, this featured the charismatic teacher revealing a gnostic secret. Known as the Positive Confession or Word of Faith movement, it was, in a sense, more democratic than its predecessor because anyone with an ear to hear could appropriate and apply the deeper truths unearthed by the movement's teachers.

Until his death in 2003, Texas-born Kenneth Hagin, Sr., towered over the movement as its unquestioned patriarch. A former AG minister and Gordon Lindsay associate, Hagin left the AG in the mid-1960s to form Kenneth E. Hagin Evangelistic Association, eventually settling in Tulsa, Oklahoma. In 1974 he founded Rhema Bible Training Center in nearby Broken Arrow. Under Hagin's tutelage, the Positive Confession movement grew rapidly throughout the 1980s and 1990s, boosted by the *RHEMA Praise* program on TBN and a daily radio program, *Faith Seminar of the Air*. Together with his son and successor, Kenneth Hagin, Jr., he penned more than a hundred books and published a monthly magazine, *The Word of Faith*. Yet, Hagin's Bible Training Center provided the true engine of the movement. By 2010, almost 25,000 Rhema graduates had planted over 1,500 congregations worldwide.

Hagin's son inherited his ministry, but fellow Texan Kenneth Copeland proved to be his most gifted and influential protégé. A talented singer-musician and former recording artist like Swaggart, Copeland teamed with his wife Gloria to found a Word of Faith ministry that has rivaled or surpassed that of his mentor. Copeland's *Believers Voice of Victory* television program aired on almost 500 stations worldwide in 2010, while his monthly magazine of the same name claimed a circulation of a half million. Other leaders of note within the movement included the aptly named Price and Dollar, and until his fall in the 1990s, Robert Tilton.

Much variety of emphasis now exists within Positive Confession, but its theological foundation still rests on its explication of Christian anthropology, particularly the doctrine of *imago dei*. The central epiphany of Positive Confession, then, springs from the full realization of what it means to be made in the image and likeness of God, and from the corresponding recognition that God wills prosperity of spirit, soul, and body for God's children. However, the movement teaches that God's will must be realized through "positive" confession, a potent act that creates the reality it confesses according to laws of faith that are as certain and reliable as those of physics. Such is the power of the spoken word—the *rhema*—when it originates in Holy Ghost revelation and is uttered through unwavering faith in accordance with the will of God and the laws of the divine economy as outlined in the written Word of Holy Scripture. In short, the child of God can speak into being anything that is consistent with the will of God.[22]

Those who embrace this teaching have found an exhilarating sense of mysteries revealed and latent power unleashed, which helps to explain its extraordinary appeal. Like other zones of convergence, it has become a vital crossroads for classical Pentecostalism and the charismatic movement in the United States and even abroad, where it is represented by global celebrities like German evangelist Reinhard Bonnke, Ray McCauley of South Africa, and Ulf Eckman of Sweden. The full magnitude of the movement is difficult to estimate, given the independent nature of Word of Faith churches and ministries. But Rhema Ministerial Association International alone now credentials 2,000 ministers who pastor almost 900 churches in the United States. Overall figures for the movement are sure to be much higher.

NAME BRAND BELIEVERS

As Pentecostalism moves further into the 21st century, dynamism and rates of growth seem greatest in the unfettered open spaces, where independent Pentecostals and charismatics mingle promiscuously and celebrate their spiritual liberty in creative ways. But Pentecostal denominations have remained the backbone of the movement, providing structure, discipline, accountability, and focus, along with some creative liberty of their own.

The Assemblies of God still stands as the movement's leading denomination in status, wealth, influence, visibility, quite likely in U.S. adherence, and certainly in global adherence. As such it provides an important weathervane of American Pentecostalism. Over the past 40 years, the trend toward bureaucratic efficiency described in the previous chapter continued in the AG, as it did in virtually all Pentecostal denominations. Yet routinization did not extinguish charisma, as the Brownsville revival amply demonstrates. At times, the AG has in fact seemed to capture lightening in a bottle. From the mid-1970s to the mid-1990s, for example, it posted a 17 percent rate of annual increase, making it the most rapidly growing denomination in the United States over that period. Its outreach to minority constituents proved especially successful, with growth in its Korean district, added in 1981, surpassed only by that among its Hispanic members. Indeed, by the late 1980s, Hispanics composed 15 percent of the denomination's constituency.

In 1985, the Thomas Zimmerman era came to a close. Since then, executive leadership has passed hands more frequently: to G. Raymond Carlson in 1985, Thomas Trask in 1993, and George O. Wood in 2007. Despite the denomination's notable successes, however, leaders have called attention to areas of concern. Growth in U.S. adherence has slowed since the mid-1990s, leveling off at an average annual increase of just over 1 percent between 2003 and 2008. Churches have also seen declines in Sunday school attendance and attendance at midweek and evening services. Moreover, the tradition of holding altar services and prayer meetings has faded.

Many of these trends, however, are simply by-products of the denomination's growing acculturation. Together with the Four-square Church, the AG has set the pace for clothing the gospel in the accoutrements of contemporary culture. But acculturation has not come without a price, and recent years have witnessed a renewed search for identity within the AG. Since the 1980s, an increasing number of its ministers have been trained at evangelical institutions like Fuller Theological Seminary, Gordon-Conwell, and Trinity Evangelical Divinity School. This option has become all the more inviting as Pentecostals have risen to positions of leadership at those very schools.

In some cases, however, evangelical education has led to greater doctrinal latitude and, in particular, to weakened support for the doctrine of initial evidence. Alarmed by these trends, leaders have challenged members to recover a distinctive Pentecostal identity and thus remain more than "evangelicals plus."[23] Denominational authorities have also sought to tighten the ordination process and to exercise greater scrutiny over textbooks used in AG colleges and secondary schools. Despite these efforts, the trend toward greater affinity with other evangelicals has continued.

Another concern has risen from the tensions inherent to a denomination stretched between the haves and the have-nots, the megachurch and the median congregation. Studies suggest that at least half of all AG congregations average less than a hundred in weekly attendance. Despite these areas of concern, however, the Assemblies of God is now firmly planted in the ranks of America's leading Protestant bodies, with almost three million adherents and more than 12,000 churches in the United States in 2010.[24]

Reformed or Finished Work denominations like the AG, the Four-square Church, the PCG, and the Open Bible Churches have always had the easier path to mainstream Protestant culture because of their conformity to generic evangelical orthodoxy. Yet Holiness and Oneness denominations have also enjoyed robust growth in recent decades, whether in spite of or because of their relatively high boundaries and their greater preservation of Pentecostal distinctives in dress, manners, and style of worship.

The largest Holiness denomination, the Church of God in Christ, has outgrown its Southern roots to become a truly national body. In many of America's inner cities, it now stands as the leading organized religious force. The rapid expansion of the black middle class after the 1960s, moreover, brought rising affluence, prestige, resources, and political influence to the denomination, which enabled it to play a leading role in the Pentecostalization of the larger Black Church. As with the AG, numerical growth has corresponded with rising acculturation and bureaucratic regularity, as evidenced by the 2007 election of Charles Edward Blake, pastor of West Angeles Church of God in Christ, as presiding bishop of the COGIC. Bishop Blake's election marked both the most democratic transition in the denomination's history and an important symbolic step toward greater openness and social engagement. In 2010, the COGIC claimed six and a half million U.S. adherents. Demographers may view that figure with some suspicion,[25] but the rapid growth and impressive size of the denomination lie beyond dispute.[26]

The Church of God (Cleveland, Tennessee) has set the bar for predominately white Holiness bodies, with approximately one million four hundred thousand adherents in 2010. Particularly since the 1980s, that growth has correlated with greater openness to the world beyond its denominational borders. Along the way, the COG has continued the process of racial reconciliation begun in the 1960s, electing an African American to head its Evangelism and Home Mission department in 2006, the first nonwhite to fill an office of that kind.[27] Other Holiness Pentecostal bodies have experienced similar success, with the Pentecostal Holiness Church boosting its membership by more than 50 percent over the course of the 1990s. Recent decades proved less auspicious for the Church of God of Prophecy, where financial losses and a change in leadership brought declines in membership, but the denomination has regrouped and appears to have stabilized its course.

More than any other branch, Oneness Pentecostals have carried forward the movement's historic emphasis on separation from the world. At the beginning of the 21st century, even the largest Oneness body, the United Pentecostal Church, still forbade short hair and the wearing of pants for women and discouraged television ownership among its clergy. Nevertheless, Oneness Pentecostals have also changed with the times. The ecumenical impulse has brought many Oneness groups together under the rubric of the Apostolic World Christian Fellowship, founded in 1971, and intercourse beyond Oneness circles has increased, particularly on the part of African American Oneness Pentecostals.

Education has also driven change within the movement. The United Pentecostal Church, for example, sponsors or endorses several Bible colleges along with a graduate school of theology, and Oneness scholars have participated in intra-Pentecostal dialogue with Reformed and Holiness peers under the auspices of the Society for Pentecostal Studies for more than 30 years.

Yet, Oneness Pentecostalism continues to distinguish itself by its abiding commitment to holiness of lifestyle and free-flowing Pentecostal worship. Furthermore, it has best preserved the interracial character of the early movement. Approximately half of all Oneness Pentecostals in the United States are nonwhite, a number that has increased with successful reverse missions by Oneness imports like the True Jesus Church (Taiwan), the Spirit of Jesus Church (Japan), and the United Pentecostal Church of Colombia. In these respects, Oneness Pentecostalism may offer 21st-century observers their best glimpse into the provocative, impassioned world of early Pentecostalism.

If Oneness Pentecostalism still stands apart from its Reformed and Holiness kin, however, it has kept pace with them in the matter of church growth. Estimates suggest well over two million Oneness believers in the United States, including 850,000 in the United Pentecostal Church and perhaps 500,000 in the Pentecostal Assemblies of the World. Additional tens of thousands are found in smaller, often ethnic bodies like the Apostolic Assembly of Faith in Christ Jesus.[28]

Pentecostal denominations, then, enter the 21st century with notable strengths and advantages. But like religious denominations everywhere, they face the existential dilemma of a postdenominational world increasingly shaped by freelance Christianity. According to one Pentecostal scholar, roughly half of all Pentecostal congregations are now independent.[29] That is not likely to change with individuals and even congregations now able to select from a smorgasbord of Pentecostal-charismatic resources and relationships to satisfy their needs or appetites.

Clearly, denominations will continue to shape Pentecostalism and to drive much of its growth in the United States and abroad. But they will be pressed to explain the value of denominational structures for 21st-century Christians. What is to be gained by trading congregational liberty for the hierarchy and bureaucracy of denominational affiliation? Do the benefits of oversight, support, brand recognition, and formal coordination offset the weight of denominational encumbrance? It will not be enough to point to past success or appeal to residual loyalty or rely on historical inertia. Pentecostal denominations must demonstrate their relevance to the local congregation, indeed, to the individual church member. They will continue to survive, of that I am sure. But will they thrive? That remains to be seen.

NOTES

1. The list of politically active Pentecostals includes William Holt (deputy sheriff in California) and Elmer Walker (cofounder of the North Dakota Non-Partisan League) in the 1910s; James G. Crites (Non-Partisan League activist and mayor of Lisbon, North Dakota), Beatrice Hooper (member of the Michigan central committee of the Prohibition Party), John Law (Justice of the Peace in Wilton, North Dakota), and S. Clyde Bailey (police chief, Marion, Illinois), all in the 1920s; and Robert L. Gibson (Democratic member of the West Virginia state legislature) in the 1930s. See Grant Wacker, *Heaven Below: Early Pentecostals and American Culture* (Cambridge, MA: Harvard University Press, 2001), 220–223; and Darrin Rodgers, *Northern Harvest: Pentecostalism in North Dakota* (Bismark: North Dakota District Council of the Assemblies of God, 2003).

2. For McPherson's political activities, see Matthew Avery Sutton, *Aimee Semple McPherson and the Resurrection of Christian America* (Cambridge, MA: Harvard University Press, 2007).

3. Assemblies of God leaders Ernest Williams and Alice Luce, quoted in Sutton, 215.

4. My account of Pentecostalism and the civil rights movement draws on Edith Blumhofer, *Restoring the Faith: The Assemblies of God, Pentecostalism, and American Culture* (Urbana: University of Illinois Press, 1993); Mickey Crews, *The Church of God: A Social History* (Knoxville: University of Tennessee Press, 1990); Eric Patterson and Edmund Rybarcyk, eds., *The Future of Pentecostalism in the United States* (Lanham, MD: Lexington Books, 2007); Randall Stephens, *The Fire Spreads: Holiness and Pentecostalism in the American South* (Cambridge, MA: Harvard University Press, 2008); Vinson Synan, *The Holiness-Pentecostal Tradition: Charismatic Movements in the Twentieth Century*, rev. ed. (Grand Rapids, MI: Wm. B. Eerdmans Publishing, 1997); and Vinson Synan, *The Century of the Holy Spirit: 100 Years of Pentecostal and Charismatic Renewal, 1901–2001* (Nashville, TN: Thomas Nelson, 2001).

5. Blumhofer, *Restoring the Faith,* 247.

6. Blumhofer, *Restoring the Faith,* 250.

7. Margaret Poloma, *The Assemblies of God at the Crossroads: Charisma and Institutional Dilemmas* (Knoxville: University of Tennessee Press, 1989), note 7, p. 281.

8. William Lindsey and Mark Silk, eds., *Religion and Public Life in the Southern Crossroads: Showdown States* (Lanham, MD: AltaMira Press, 2005), 95.

9. Survey data is taken from *Spirit and Power: A 10-Country Survey of Pentecostals* (Washington, DC: Pew Forum on Religion and the Public Life, October 2006), 36–39, 61–72, 94; and *U.S. Religious Landscape Survey: Religious Beliefs and Practices: Diverse and Politically Relevant* (Washington, DC: Pew Forum on Religion and the Public Life, June 2008), 135–143; 150–152. See also Gregory Smith, "Palin V. P. Nomination Puts Pentecostalism in the Spotlight," (Washington, DC: Pew Forum on Religion and the Public Life, September, 2008).

10. For insights into Pentecostals and politics, in addition to sources listed above, see David Edwin Harrell, Jr., *Pat Robertson: A Personal, Religious, and Political Portrait* (New York: Harper & Row, 1987); Corwin Smidt, Lyman Kellstedt, John Green, and James Guth, "The Spirit-Filled Movements in Contemporary America: A Survey Perspective," in *Pentecostal Currents in American Protestantism*, eds. Edith Blumhofer, Russell Spittler, and Grant Wacker (Urbana: University of Illinois Press, 1999); and Donald Miller and Tetsunao Yamamori, *Global Pentecostalism: The New Face of Christian Social Engagement* (Berkeley: University of California Press, 2007).

11. Synan, *Century of the Holy Spirit*, 11.

12. See Smidt, Kellstedt, Green, and Guth, 114.

13. For a brief history of the Vineyard movement, see Donald Miller, *Reinventing American Protestantism: Christianity in the New Millennium* (Berkeley: University of California Press, 1997).

14. Rich Nathan and Ken Wilson, *Empowered Evangelicals: Bringing Together the Best of the Evangelical and Charismatic Worlds* (Ann Arbor, MI: Vine Books, 1995).

15. Roger Robins, personal communication with Berten Waggoner, February 8, 2010. Waggoner points out that, although the Vineyard eschews the initial evidence shibboleth, glossolalia is more widely practiced in the Vineyard than in the AG.

16. Smidt, Kellstedt, Green, and Guth, 116.

17. Quotation taken from FGBCF Web site: http://www.fullgospel baptist.org.

18. Kenneth Woodward, "The Giggles Are for God," *Newsweek*, February 20, 1995; and Leslie Scrivener, *Toronto Star*, October 8, 1995.

19. For the Latin American axis of this phenomenon, see Arlene Sanchez Walsh and Eric Patterson, "Latino Pentecostalism: Globalized

Christianity and the United States," in *The Future of Pentecostalism in the United States*, eds. Eric Patterson and Edmund Rybarcyk (Lanham, MD: Lexington Books, 2007), chapter 5.

20. For Bakker and Swaggart, see Synan, *Century of the Holy Spirit*; entries in Stanley Burgess and Eduard van der Mass, eds., *The International Dictionary of Pentecostal and Charismatic Movements*, rev. ed. (Grand Rapids, MI: Zondervan, 2003); and David E. Harrell, Jr., "Swaggart, Jimmy Lee," in *Biographical Dictionary of Evangelicals*, eds. Timothy Larsen, David Bebbington, and Mark Noll (Downers Grove, IL: InterVarsity Press, 2003).

21. Blumhofer, *Restoring the Faith*, 255.

22. Key proof-texts include Psalm 35:27 ("The Lord...delights in the prosperity of his servant"); Mark 11:24 ("what things soever ye desire, when ye pray, believe that ye receive them, and ye shall have them"); and 3 John 2 (he "calleth those things which be not as though they were").

23. See Thomas Trask, *Back to the Altar: A Call to Spiritual Awakening* (Springfield, MO: Gospel Publishing House, 1994).

24. For the recent history of the Assemblies of God, see Gary B. McGee, *People of the Spirit: The Assemblies of God* (Springfield, MO: Gospel Publishing House, 2004); and Edith Blumhofer, *The Assemblies of God: A Chapter in the Story of American Pentecostalism*, Vol. 2 (Springfield, MO: Gospel Publishing House, 1989).

25. Methods of tabulation appear to have changed between 1965, when the denomination reported 425,000 adherents, and 1973, when it reported 3 million. This represented a sevenfold increase in an eight-year span. Since then, self-reported figures for COGIC, like those for other black Pentecostal denominations, have fallen significantly outside projections based on survey data. For example, the 2008 Pew *U.S. Religious Landscape* survey estimated a total of 2.7 million African American Pentecostals in the United States. However, it is important to note that COGIC figures are merely symptomatic of self-reported adherence within the Black Church generally. For example, the *World Christian Encyclopedia*, 2nd ed. (New York: Oxford University Press, 2001), drawing on self-reported World Religion Database figures, gave a 1995 adherence of 34.7 million for the top 12 black Protestant denominations alone, which exceeded the nation's total estimated black population by almost 2 million. Based on those figures, furthermore, just the top 3 predominately black Pentecostal bodies claimed adherence equal to an unlikely 22 percent of all black Americans.

26. For a recent prospectus of the Church of God in Christ, see David Daniels, "Follow Peace with All: Future Trajectories in the Church of God in Christ," in *The Future of Pentecostalism*, eds. Patterson and Rybarcyk, chapter 12.

27. For recent developments in the Church of God (Cleveland, Tennessee), see Kimberly Ervin Alexander, "The Almost Pentecostals: The Future of the Church of God in the United States," in *The Future of Pentecostalism*, eds. Patterson and Rybarcyk, chapter 9.

28. For Oneness Pentecostalism, see David A. Reed, *"In Jesus' Name": The History and Beliefs of Oneness Pentecostals* (Blandford Forum, UK: Deo Publishing, 2008); and David K. Bernard, "The Future of Oneness Pentecostalism," in *The Future of Pentecostalism*, eds. Patterson and Rybarcyk, chapter 8.

29. Synan, *Century of the Holy Spirit*, 351.

Conclusion

As a new century enters its teens, Pentecostalism looks back on an extraordinary record of growth and change. Early skeptics often ignored the movement with the expectation that it would go away. Such a response would now be unthinkable. Pentecostalism has burgeoned into a prominent and permanent feature of modern America. The best recent surveys put the number of classical Pentecostals at about 5 percent of the population, or approximately 15 million people. But those estimates are conservative, and the true number could run much higher. When the survey net is cast most widely, to include all renewalists—Pentecostals, charismatics, and neo-charismatics—the count swells to as high as 76 million Americans. In fact, one recent survey reported that over one-third of U.S. adults now fall into the renewalist category. Those numbers pale in comparison to the ones found on the global scene, however, where World Religion Database figures list over 600 million renewalists worldwide, including between 80 and 90 million classical Pentecostals.[1]

Pentecostalism has leapt, lurched, and bounded to these startling heights in scarcely more than a single century. It can now be found in every reach of America, from heartland to borderland. Like Proteus, it takes seemingly infinite forms. It is the garish megachurch, the dim urban storefront, and the modest hillside chapel. It is upper class and underclass, immigrant and native-born. It appears in scores of languages and in every hue of the human rainbow. And in all of these forms, it is tightly woven into the social and religious tapestry of the nation.

ISSUES AND CHALLENGES

Pentecostalism faces many issues and challenges—some old, others new—as it steps further into the 21st century. One of the most important has to do with the role of women in ministry, an old issue that has acquired a new twist. Two decades ago, Margaret Poloma found that younger pastors in the Assemblies of God (AG) were less supportive of ordaining women than were their older and otherwise more ethically rigorist peers.[2] This suggested that rapprochement with evangelicalism might be eroding support for women in the ministry. In the 20 years since, however, formal barriers against the ordination of women have actually lowered in most Pentecostal denominations.

Yet a curious paradox has surfaced. As ecclesiastical hurdles have fallen, the percentage of women in ordained ministry has actually declined. Even the Mount Sinai Holy Church of North America, where 70 percent of all ministers were women as late as the 1970s, saw the tables turn in the late 1980s, so that now a majority of its ministers, including its current president, are men. One possibility is that Pentecostal engagement in the struggle against radical feminism has tilted the cultural mood against women in nontraditional roles, even as the legal climate has grown more permissive. Of course, to speak of a more permissive legal climate is to elide "exceptional" sectors of Pentecostalism, including several smaller bodies shaped by more patriarchal immigrant or ethnic cultures, where the ordination of women is still simply forbidden.

Race presents another old issue with a new twist. After long decades of viewing race primarily in terms of black and white, Pentecostals now confront a demographic future that sees Hispanics and Asians rising to the fore of the movement. Since the 1980s, the growth of American Pentecostalism has been especially indebted to its success among Hispanics; indeed, a 2007 Pew survey found that approximately one-third of Protestant Hispanics in the United States are now Pentecostal.[3] Furthermore, this growth has been accompanied by increasing Hispanic diversity, as immigrants from South and Central America and the Caribbean join older generations of Mexican Americans in the melting pot or salad bowl of American Pentecostalism. Although many Asian and Hispanic Pentecostals have found homes within independent congregations or ethnic-majority denominations, all of the major historic bodies now have large Hispanic and Asian contingents.

The issue of race intersects with the remarkable spread of Pentecostalism abroad, where explosive growth has dwarfed that within the United States. Many Pentecostal denominations now report ratios of foreign to U.S. adherence well in excess of 10 to 1. To give three examples, the AG reports 60 million foreign adherents to only 3 million in the United States; the Foursquare Church reports over 8 million foreign to 350,000 U.S. followers; while the Pentecostal Holiness Church reports 4 million foreign adherents to 340,000 in the United States. Both the increasing diversity of American Pentecostalism and the predominately non-American—indeed non-Western—character of global Pentecostalism raise compelling questions about Pentecostal identity. White American Pentecostals, in particular, must reframe their images of self and other to match the transformed reality of the movement of which they are a part.

The continuing process of assimilation is forcing Pentecostals to address another aspect of core identity. As Pentecostals file into the evangelical wing of the American mainstream, once-cherished symbolic markers have begun to fall away. In 2001, the AG liberalized one of its oldest distinguishing strictures: its refusal to issue credentials to divorced ministers who remarry while a former spouse still lives. And groups like the AG and the Foursquare Church have long since abandoned the old Holiness-inspired restrictions on dress and secular pastimes. In addition, they have fielded Christian versions of virtually every aspect of mainstream popular culture. For example, visitors to the Latin American Bible Institute—once a bastion of conservative dress—now find students garbed in earrings, baggy pants, and dyed hair or shaved heads praising God to the latest strains of Christian rap and rock.[4] Similar trends are transforming even more resistant bodies, such as the Church of God (Cleveland, Tennessee), the Pentecostal Church of God, and the Church of God of Prophecy.

Another measure of acculturation has been the quantity and quality of scholarship produced within the movement. Since its founding in 1970, the Society for Pentecostal Studies has provided a welcome outlet for Pentecostal scholars, many of whom spent their early careers sailing into strong anti-intellectual headwinds. It was also the first organization to bring Trinitarian and Oneness Pentecostals together and now provides a forum for dialogue across the full range of the Pentecostal–charismatic spectrum. In fact, charismatic scholars have twice been elected to preside over the society. In addition, *PNEUMA: The Journal for the Society of Pentecostal Studies* has made important contributions to scholarship by and about Pentecostals.

Pentecostal scholarship has paid especially rich dividends in the field of religious history. Sympathetic outsiders like John Thomas Nichol and Robert Anderson and Europeans like Walter Hollenwegger and Nils Bloch-Hoell once produced the best scholarly accounts of Pentacostalism, but the leading works now come from historians and social scientists with roots inside the movement. Since the 1980s, scholars such as Edith Blumhofer, Vinson Synan, and Grant Wacker have taken command of the movement's narrative, aided by a circle of younger historians like Dan Ramirez, Anthea Butler, David Daniels, and Arlene Sánchez-Walsh. Pentecostals have also risen to prominence in the fields of ethics, biblical studies, and theology. Here the list includes Robert Cooley, Gordon Fee, Robert Franklin, Veli-Matti Kärkkäinen, Peter Kuzmic, Mel Robeck, Cheryl Sanders, Russell Spittler, Eldin Villafañe, and Mirsoslav Volf.

Yet distinction in the world of mainstream scholarship raises its own vexing questions, particularly for scholars working outside the fields of theology and religious studies or at secular institutions. To what extent can one adhere to the canons of the secular academy while remaining true to the foundational assumptions of Pentecostalism? Is it possible to achieve excellence as measured by the criteria of the academy without subtly (or not so subtly) suspending the core elements of a Pentecostal worldview? Should Pentecostal scholarship instead be erected on its own presuppositional scaffolding, and according to its own distinctive sources and criteria?

Like so many sectarians before them, then, Pentecostals have discovered that acculturation is a bittersweet pilgrimage; it is, in its own way, a form of immigration. As Pentecostals move deeper into the 21st century, therefore, they will continue to grapple with the question Thomas Trask posed more than a decade ago: How can Pentecostals today be "evangelical" and yet maintain a distinctive Pentecostal identity? Naturally, they will ask the question in their own way, searching to determine which of the elements of their heritage are essential and which superficial under the light of Holy Scripture. But from the perspective of social psychology, we might frame it somewhat differently. How much of their past do Pentecostals need to preserve in order to remember who they are? How can they make their way in a world they now choose to be a part of, while yet preserving the inner sense that sustained them over so many generations: the sense of being a people set apart? It is not wrong for a subculture to pass from outside to inside the social mainstream. But it is psychologically treacherous to do so.

The most pressing issue confronting Pentecostals in the 21st century, however, concerns the movement's use of its increasing wealth, social influence, and political power. Matthew 16:26 has always been a favored Pentecostal verse: "For what is a man profited, if he shall gain the whole world, and lose his own soul?" Pentecostals will have to ask if it is possible to gain both without losing either. The recent political turn will draw Pentecostals into a morass of quandaries. Politics requires compromise, half-measures, even unsavory alliances in the pursuit of relative goods. Are Pentecostals willing to surrender perfectionism for the sake of effectiveness? And which relative goods will they pursue? Common goods to be shared by the whole of a pluralistic democracy or particular goods that serve more narrow Pentecostal or evangelical interests? These are the questions that will measure the character of Pentecostalism in the new millennium.

A PARTING WORD

We have watched Pentecostalism expand and evolve over the decades, spawning or influencing other movements, only to be influenced by them in turn. Our focus has remained on classical Pentecostalism, but we have seen that, by the 21st century, rigid distinctions between the movement and its many kindred spirits had become difficult, if not impossible, to maintain. Those seeking the face of contemporary Pentecostalism, then, will find not a crisp image reflected off a looking glass but a shifting figure on the surface of a wishing pool.

Even when we simplify, move in from the margins, and paint with broad strokes, classical Pentecostalism remains striking for its diversity. I have outlined the doctrinal divisions that formed the movement's Holiness, Oneness, and Finished Work branches, but I have not delved deeply into many of the other, often arcane points of division. It is not that kind of book. But in fact many additional fault lines do transect classical Pentecostalism, cutting across and between the three main branches. There are ecclesiological differences. Some Pentecostals fiercely guard their independence. Others form associations, but Baptist-like, in the congregational style. The Wesleyan heritage has led many to episcopal polity, while still others have adopted presbyterian forms of governance. Some still speak the language of theocracy. There are eschatological disputes as well, with groups parsing dispensationalism in different ways. And then, of course, there are the racial, cultural, and political divides that we have already observed. Many congregations are racially integrated, but most are predominately white, black, Hispanic, or Asian. Pentecostal worship ranges from eye-popping ecstasy to stately grace. Some Pentecostals are fully assimilated; others still entrenched in their

Table 1

Selected List of Leading or Historic Denominations in the Classical Tradition

Name and Branch of Pentecostalism	Headquarters	2010 Estimated Adherence[a]
Apostolic Assemblies of the Faith in Christ Jesus (Asamblea Apostólica de la Fe en Cristo Jesus) [Holiness Pentecostal]	10807 Laurel Street, Rancho Cucamonga, CA 91730	75,000
General Council of the Assemblies of God [Reformed Pentecostal]	1445 N Boonville Avenue, Springfield, MO 65802	2,970,000
Assemblies of the Lord Jesus Christ [Oneness Pentecostal]	875 N White Station Road, Memphis, TN 38122	50,000[b]
International Bible Way Church of Jesus Christ [Oneness Pentecostal]	27 South Caroline Street, Baltimore, MD 21231	70,000
Church of God in Christ [Holiness Pentecostal]	930 Mason Street, Memphis, TN 38126	6,500,000[c]
Church of God (Cleveland, Tennessee) [Holiness Pentecostal]	2490 Keith Street, Cleveland, TN 37320	1,400,000
Church of God of Prophecy [Holiness Pentecostal]	3720 Keith Street, Cleveland, TN 37320	90,000
International Church of the Foursquare Gospel (Foursquare Church) [Reformed Pentecostal]	1910 W Sunset Boulevard, Los Angeles, CA 90026	350,000
International Pentecostal Holiness Church [Holiness Pentecostal]	7300 NW 39th Expressway, Bethany, OK 73008	340,000
Mt. Sinai Holy Church of North America [Holiness Pentecostal]	1469 N Broad Street Philadelphia, PA 19122	50,000
Open Bible Churches [Reformed Pentecostal]	2020 Bell Avenue, Des Moines, IA 50315	30,000
Pentecostal Assemblies of the World [Oneness Pentecostal]	3939 N Meadows Drive, Indianapolis, IN 46205	500,000
Pentecostal Church of God Inc. [Reformed Pentecostal]	4901 Pennsylvania Avenue, Joplin, MO 64804	100,000

(Continued)

Table 1
(*Continued*)

Name and Branch of Pentecostalism	Headquarters	2010 Estimated Adherence[a]
Rhema Ministerial Association International [Reformed/ Word of Faith Pentecostal]	1025 W Kenosha Street, Broken Arrow, OK 74012	150,000
United Holy Church of America, Inc. [Holiness Pentecostal]	5140 Dunstan Road, Greensboro, NC 27405	50,000
United Pentecostal Church International [Oneness Pentecostal]	8855 Dunn Road, Hazelwood, MO 63042	850,000

[a]Best available 2010 estimates based on telephone interviews and published sources, including denominational Web sites and David Barrett, George Kurian, and Todd Johnson, eds., *World Christian Encyclopedia*, 2nd ed. (New York: Oxford University Press, 2001); Dale Jones, Sherri Doty, et al., *Religious Congregations and Membership in the United States 2000* (Cincinnati, OH: Glenmary Research Center, 2002); Frank Mead and Samuel Hill, *Handbook of Denominations in the United States*, 11th ed. (Nashville, TN: Abingdon Press, 2001); and William Newman and Peter Halvarsen, *Atlas of American Religion: The Denominational Era, 1776–1990* (Lanham, MD: AltaMira Press, 2000). Figures for Pentecostal Assemblies of the World are based on David A. Reed, *"In Jesus' Name": The History and Beliefs of Oneness Pentecostals* (Blandford Forum, UK: Deo Publishing, 2008), 221.

[b]Extrapolated from number of churches based on average membership per congregation reported in 1997.

[c]Author's notice: low confidence figure.

sectarian outposts. Pentecostals are Republican, Democratic, independent, and, yes, still apolitical. Some warmly embrace their charismatic cousins; others keep a guarded distance.

Yet for all these many differences, threads of coherence spun by a common past, a distinctive practice, and shared religious assumptions still bind classical Pentecostalism together. In fact, a singular conviction prevails across the movement in its broad entirety. The power of first-century Christianity, Pentecostals believe, is as real today as ever. God has not aged nor has the Holy Spirit weakened over those 2,000 years. Jesus Christ remains the same yesterday, today, and forever. Because of that conviction, Pentecostals inhabit a world that is alive with divine promise. Should you find yourself alone with Pentecostal neighbors, colleagues, or friends, be forewarned. They may feel compelled to explain that, by the power of God, something good could happen to *you*.

NOTES

1. Statistical data drawn from *U.S. Religious Landscape Survey: Religious Beliefs and Practices: Diverse and Politically Relevant* (Washington, DC: Pew Forum on Religion and the Public Life, June 2008); *Spirit and Power: A 10-Country Survey of Pentecostals* (Washington, DC: Pew Forum on Religion and the Public Life, October 2006); Todd Johnson and Kenneth Ross, *Atlas of Global Christianity* (Edinburgh, Scotland: Edinburgh University Press, 2009); "Is American Christianity Turning Charismatic?" (Ventura, CA: Barna Group) January 7, 2008; and *International Bulletin of Missionary Research,* January 2010.

2. Margaret Poloma, *The Assemblies of God at the Crossroads: Charisma and Institutional Dilemmas* (Knoxville: University of Tennessee Press, 1989).

3. *Changing Faith: Latinos and the Transformation of American Religion* (Washington, DC: Pew Hispanic Center and Pew Forum on Religion & Public Life, 2007).

4. Arlene Sánchez Walsh, *Latino Pentecostal Identity: Evangelical Faith, Self, and Society* (New York: Columbia University Press, 2003), 81.

Bibliography

Alexander, Paul. *Peace to War: Shifting Allegiances in the Assemblies of God.* Telford, PA: Cascadia Publishing House, 2009.

Anderson, Allan. *An Introduction to Pentecostalism: Global Charismatic Christianity.* Cambridge: Cambridge University Press, 2004.

Anderson, Robert. *Vision of the Disinherited: The Making of American Pentecostalism.* New York: Oxford University Press, 1979.

Blumhofer, Edith. *Aimee Semple McPherson: Everybody's Sister.* Grand Rapids, MI: Wm. B. Eerdmans Publishing, 1993.

Blumhofer, Edith. *Restoring the Faith: The Assemblies of God, Pentecostalism, and American Culture.* Urbana: University of Illinois Press, 1993.

Blumhofer, Edith, Russell Spittler, and Grant Wacker, eds. *Pentecostal Currents in American Protestantism.* Urbana: University of Illinois Press, 1999.

Burgess, Stanley, and Eduard Van Der Maas, eds. *The New International Dictionary of Pentecostal and Charismatic Movements,* rev. ed. Grand Rapids, MI: Zondervan, 2003.

Cox, Harvey. *Fire from Heaven: The Rise of Pentecostal Spirituality and the Reshaping of Religion in the 21st Century.* Reading, MA: Addison-Wesley, 1995.

Goff, James, Jr. *Fields White unto Harvest: Charles F. Parham and the Missionary Origins of Pentecostalism.* Fayetteville: University of Arkansas Press, 1988.

Harrell, David Edwin Jr. *All Things Are Possible: The Healing and Charismatic Revivals in Modern America.* Bloomington: Indiana University Press, 1975.

Harrell, David Edwin Jr. *Oral Roberts: An American Life.* Bloomington: Indiana University Press, 1985.

Harrell, David Edwin Jr. *Pat Robertson: A Personal, Religious, and Political Portrait.* New York: Harper & Row, 1987.

Hollenweger, Walter J. *Pentecostalism: Origins and Development Worldwide.* Peabody, MA: Hendrickson Publishers, 1997.

McGee, Gary B. *People of the Spirit: The Assemblies of God.* Springfield, MO: Gospel Publishing House, 2004.

Miller, Donald. *Reinventing American Protestantism: Christianity in the New Millennium.* Berkeley: University of California Press, 1997.

Miller, Donald, and Tetsunao Yamamori. *Global Pentecostalism: The New Face of Christian Social Engagement.* Berkeley: University of California Press, 2007.

Patterson, Eric, and Edmund Rybarcyk, eds. *The Future of Pentecostalism in the United States.* Lanham, MD: Lexington Books, 2007.

Poloma, Margaret. *The Assemblies of God at the Crossroads: Charisma and Institutional Dilemmas.* Knoxville: University of Tennessee Press, 1989.

Poloma, Margaret. *Main Street Mystics: The Toronto Blessing and Reviving Pentecostalism.* Lanham, MD: AltaMira Press, 2003.

Quebedeaux, Richard. *The New Charismatics II.* New York: Harper & Row, 1983.

Reed, David A. *"In Jesus' Name": The History and Beliefs of Oneness Pentecostals.* Blandford Forum, UK: Deo Publishing, 2008.

Robeck, Cecil M. Jr. *The Azusa Street Mission and Revival.* Nashville, TN: Thomas Nelson, 2006.

Robins, Roger Glenn. *A. J. Tomlinson: Plainfolk Modernist.* New York: Oxford University Press, 2004.

Sánchez-Walsh, Arlene. *Latino Pentecostal Identity: Evangelical Faith, Self, and Society.* New York: Columbia University Press, 2003.

Stephens, Randall. *The Fire Spreads: Holiness and Pentecostalism in the American South.* Cambridge, MA: Harvard University Press, 2008.

Sutton, Matthew. *Aimee Semple McPherson and the Resurrection of Christian America.* Cambridge, MA: Harvard University Press, 2007.

Synan, Vinson. *The Century of the Holy Spirit: 100 Years of Pentecostal and Charismatic Renewal, 1901–2001.* Nashville, TN: Thomas Nelson, 2001.

Synan, Vinson. *The Holiness-Pentecostal Tradition: Charismatic Movements in the Twentieth Century*, rev. ed. Grand Rapids, MI: Wm. B. Eerdmans Publishing, 1997.

Wacker, Grant. *Heaven Below: Early Pentecostals and American Culture.* Cambridge, MA: Harvard University Press, 2001.

Wacker, Grant, and James Goff, Jr., eds., *Portraits of a Generation: Early Pentecostal Leaders.* Fayetteville: University of Arkansas Press, 2002.

Index

Adams, Leonard P., 34, 45
African-American Fire-Baptized
    Holiness Church, 44
Allen, Asa Alonso, 84–86, 88, 89,
    99, 110
Angelus Temple, 61
Anti-denominationalism, 15, 24,
    42–43, 45, 46, 65, 80, 84, 85
Apostolic Assemblies of Faith
    in Christ Jesus (Asamblea
    Apostólica de la Fe en Cristo
    Jesús), 46, 65, 76, 100, 135
Apostolic Faith (Baxter Springs),
    17, 22, 36
Apostolic Faith (Los Angeles), 37
Apostolic Faith (Portland), 37
Apostolic Faith Mission, 26–31,
    33–34, 35, 37, 38, 39, 40, 66, 125
Apostolic Faith Movement
    (Seymour), 30, 37
Apostolic Faith Movement
    (Crawford), 37, 44, 65

Apostolic Faith Movement
    (Parham), 24–28, 30, 36
Apostolic Overcoming Holy
    Church of God, 46
Ashcroft, John, 113
Assemblies of God. *See* General
    Council of the Assemblies of
    God
Assimilation. *See* Pentecostal
    acculturation
Azusa Street Mission. *See*
    Apostolic Faith Mission

Bakker, Jim, 89, 115, 126–29
Baptism with the Holy Ghost: in
    Holiness, 4–5; in Pentecostal-
    ism, 23–24, 26, 30, 31
Bartleman, Frank, 25, 26, 27, 29,
    30, 33, 53–54, 55, 58, 66
Baxter, Ern, 83, 95
Bell, Eudorus N., 36, 39, 45, 53,
    54, 55

Bennett, Dennis, 92, 120
Bible Way Churches of Our Lord
  Jesus Christ World Wide, 100
Black Church, Neo-
  Pentecostalization of, 106,
  123, 134
Black Pentecostalism. *See*
  Pentecostalism, African-
  American
Blake, Charles Edward, 134
Boardman, William, 2, 4, 5
Bosworth, Fred Francis, 46, 66,
  81, 83
Branham, William, 82–84, 85,
  86, 87
Bredeson, Harald, 91, 92, 95
Brick and mortar Pentecostalism.
  See Institutionalization
Bright, Bill, 78, 87, 114, 116
Brinkman, George, 34, 65
Britton, Francis Marion, 34, 41
Brownsville Assemblies of God,
  126
Bureaucratization. *See* Institu-
  tionalization.
Burgess-Brown, Marie, 34, 35, 39

Camp meetings, 3, 4, 17, 35, 36,
  37, 40, 80, 125
Carothers, W. Faye, 36, 38
Cashwell, Gaston Barnabas, 33,
  34, 37, 38, 43, 44
Charismatic movement, 91–93;
  and relation to classical Pente-
  costalism, 93–96
Christ for the Nations, Inc., 90, 91
Christian America, 68, 109, 112,
  115
Christian and Missionary Alli-
  ance, 4, 7, 10, 17, 35, 45
Christian Catholic Church. *See*
  Dowie, John Alexander

Christian Growth Ministries. *See*
  Discipleship movement
Christian Perfection. *See* Sanctification
Church of God (Cleveland,
  Tennessee), 17, 34, 43, 44, 45,
  69, 76, 77, 109, 143; ecclesiology
  of, 41–42; 1923 split, 63;
  statistics related to, 46, 100,
  134
Church of God, Mountain As-
  sembly, 34
Church of God of Prophecy, 63,
  64, 66, 77, 110, 134, 143
Church of God in Christ, 10, 17,
  25, 34, 43, 67, 20; and Civil
  Rights movement, 110–11;
  statistics related to, 100, 134,
  138n.25
Church of the Nazarene, 10, 17,
  33, 92
Church of Our Lord Jesus Christ
  of the Apostolic Faith, 64,
  100
Civil Religion, 68, 119
Civil Rights, Pentecostalism and,
  109–12
Class antagonism. *See* Social
  class
Colleges and universities. *See*
  Education, Pentecostal
Comeouters. *See* Independent
  bodies
Convergence, zones of (Pente-
  costal and charismatic), 95–99,
  120–26
Cook, Glenn, 35, 41
Copeland, Kenneth, 131
Counterculture. *See* The Sixties
Crawford, Florence, 25, 37, 40,
  44, 65
Crouch, Paul, 115, 127, 129

Crumpler, Abner Backmon, 11, 12, 13, 17, 33, 44

Dancing. *See* Ecstasy, religious
Darby, John Nelson, 5
Daughtry, Herbert, 111, 117
Daughtry, Leah, 117
Deliverance movement, 80–90, 110, 130
Demography, 16, 74, 75, 142
Digital age, 108, 126
Discipleship movement, 95, 119
Dispensationalism. *See* Premillennialism, dispensational
Diving healing. *See* Healing; Deliverance movement
Dowie, John Alexander, 7, 12, 17, 21, 22, 27, 34, 45, 84
DuBois, Joshua, 117
du Plessis, David, 69, 77, 78, 91, 92, 119
Durham, William Howard, 31, 33, 34, 35, 39–40, 41, 45, 60

Ecclesiasticism. *See* Antidenominationalism
Ecstasy, religious, 11–12, 24, 25, 27, 28, 31, 32, 79, 94, 121, 125, 145
Ecumenism: 50, 69, 77–78, 91, 93; Holiness, 3, 7–8, 9; Pentecostal, 37, 46, 69, 87, 119–20, 134
Education, Pentecostals and: 66, 76, 77, 89, 115, 133, 135
Egalitarianism, 10, 11, 29
Elim, 17, 35, 45
Elim Fellowship, 80
Ensign, John, 117
Entire sanctification. *See* Sanctification
Eschatology, 6, 30, 31, 32, 50, 80, 123, 145. *See also* Premillennialism, dispensational

Evening Light. *See* Eschatology
Evening Light Saints. See Warner, Daniel
Ewart, Frank, 41
Exorcism. *See* Spiritual Warfare

Faith healing. *See* Healing; Deliverance movement
Farrow, Lucy, 25, 26
Fellowship of Christian Assemblies, 80
Finished Work doctrine, 39–40, 45
Finney, Charles, 2, 4, 87
Fire-Baptized Holiness Church, 10, 17–18, 31, 34, 44. *See also* Pentecostal Holiness Church; Irwin, Benjamin Hardin
First New Testament Church. *See* Smale, Joseph
Flower, Joseph Roswell, 34, 35, 109
Foursquare Church. *See* International Church of the Foursquare Gospel
Foursquare gospel, 61
Free Methodist Church, 3, 10, 33
Frisbee, Lonnie, 98, 99, 122
Frodsham, Stanley, 54, 80
Full Gospel Baptist Church Fellowship, 123
Full Gospel Business Men's Fellowship International, 90, 91, 95, 109
Fundamentalism, 57, 58, 59, 62, 69, 78, 92, 113

Gender. *See* Women
General Council of the Assemblies of God: acculturation of, 76, 77, 133, 142, 143; and Civil Rights movement, 109–11;

and ecumenism, 119, 120; and evangelicalism, 69, 78; global outreach of, 101, 124; and deliverance evangelists, 83–85, 91; and televangelism, 127–29, 131; origins of, 45–46; pacifism within, 53–56; and politics, 113, 116, 118; statistics related to, 100, 132–33, 143

Gimenez, John, 115

Globalization, 107, 126, 132, 141, 143

Glossolalia, 18, 21, 22, 23–24, 26, 27, 28, 29, 30, 31, 92, 93, 94, 95, 99, 105, 123, 125

Godbey, William Baxter, 12, 33

Gordon, Adoniram Judson, 4, 23

Gospel of prosperity. See Prosperity teaching

Goss, Howard, 36, 41, 45

Hagin, Kenneth, Sr., 131

Harrison, Granville, 88

Harrison, Robert, 110, 111

Hayford, Jack, 121

Haywood, Garfield Thomas, 35, 41, 46

Healing, 6–7, 13, 24, 28, 63, 91, 93

Healing Movement. See Deliverance movement

Heard, R. Dennis, 76,

Heavenly chorus, 29, 79

Hensley, George W., 45

Hibbard, Jordan Carl, 90

Holiness Church of North Carolina, 10, 12, 17, 33, 34, 44. See also Pentecostal Holiness Church

Holiness movement: antebellum Holiness, 1–2; baptism with the Holy Ghost and, 4, 24, 31; comeouters, 9–10; culture of, 7–8; dispensational premillennialism and, 5–6; ecumenicity and, 3; faith healing and, 6–7; Higher Life wing, 4–5; Holiness press, 24, 30; post Civil War Holiness, 2–4; primitivism and, 8–9. See also Radical Holiness

Holmes, Nickels John, 34, 37, 44

Holy Ghost (or Holy Spirit) baptism. See Baptism with the Holy Ghost

Holy Spirit. See Pneumatology

Hornshuh, Fred, 65

Howard-Brown, Rodney, 125

Hutchins, Julia, 26

Immigration, 107, 108, 126

Independent Assemblies of God, International, 80

Independent bodies: in Holiness, 9–11; in Pentecostalism, 79, 85, 90–91, 120, 121, 132, 135

Initial evidence, doctrine of, 23, 24, 94, 133

Inskip, John, 3

Institutionalization, 42, 46, 62–63, 66, 68, 75–77, 79, 100, 132, 134

International Church of the Foursquare Gospel, 61, 65, 68, 69, 79; and Jesus movement, 98–99, 121, 133; statistics related to 100, 143

International Holiness Union and Prayer League, 10, 17, 25

Irwin, Benjamin Hardin, 14, 17, 18, 22, 31, 44

Jakes, Thomas D., 123–24
Jesus People movement, 96–99
Johnson, Timothy, 113
Jones, Charles Price, 17, 25, 43

Kansas City Conference on
    Charismatic Renewal in the
    Churches, 120
Kenworthy, Amos, 13, 14
Kenyon, Essek William, 39
Keswick conference, 4, 5, 8
King, Joseph Hillary, 34, 44
Kingdom theology, 123
Knapp, Martin Wells, 17
Kuhlman, Kathryn, 95, 120

Lake, John Graham, 25, 34, 83
Latin American Council of
    Christian Churches, 64
Latter Rain. See Eschatology
Lawson, Clarence, 110
Lawson, Robert, 64
Lindsay, James Gordon, 34, 83,
    88, 90, 91, 131
Logos Journal, 95, 116
Lopez, Luis, 46
Lum, Clara, 37
Lupton, Levi Rakestraw, 31,
    35, 38

Machen, J. Gresham, 58
Mahan, Asa, 2, 4
Malachuk, Dan, 95, 120
Mallory, Arenia, 110, 111
Mason, Charles Harrison, 17, 43,
    45
McAlister, Robert Edward, 40
McCafferty, Burt, 53
McDonnell, Kilian, 92, 95
McPherson, Aimee Semple, 47,
    60–62, 65, 68, 79, 108–9
Meares, John L., 111

Media, Pentecostalism and, 61,
    77, 89, 126, 129–30
Megachurches, 124–25
Memphis Miracle, 111
Methodism, 2, 3, 4, 10, 22, 32, 84,
    88
Militancy, 13, 14, 51
Millenarianism, 5, 6, 16, 21, 32,
    50, 52, 53, 79, 80, 81, 84, 94, 99,
    107, 112
Miracles. See Supernaturalism;
    See also Deliverance movement
Missions activity and programs,
    15, 16, 34, 35, 53, 60, 64, 76, 90,
    94, 101, 111, 128; reverse mis-
    sions, 108, 126, 135
Modernism, 56–58, 78
Modernity, Pentecostalism and,
    8, 16, 47, 58–62, 73–74, 108,
    124
Montgomery, Carrie Judd, 7, 17,
    36, 46, 64, 81
Moody, Dwight Lyman, 4, 10
Moore, Ralph, 99
Mount Calvary Holy Church of
    America, 64
Mount Sinai Holy Church of
    America, 64, 142
Musical culture, Pentecostal, 60,
    97–98
Mysticism, Holiness, 14, 16

NAE. See National Association
    of Evangelicals
National Association of Evangel-
    icals (NAE), 69, 78, 79, 91, 119
National Camp Meeting
    Association for the Promotion
    of Christian Holiness, 3
Nationalism, Pentecostalism
    and, 50, 51, 53, 54, 55, 68, 70
Nava, Antonio Castañeda, 65

Navarro, Juan, 46
Nelson, Thomas, 11, 17, 35
Neo-charismatic renewal, 105,
    107, 141
New Order of the Latter Rain,
    79–80, 90, 95, 125
The 1960s. See The Sixties
Nixon, Richard, 109
North Avenue Mission. See
    Durham, William Howard

Olazábal, Francisco, 64
Oneness controversy, 40–41,
    45–46
Open Bible Standard Church
    (Open Bible Churches), 65, 69,
    133
Opperman, Daniel C. O., 34, 41,
    45, 46
Oral Roberts University, 77, 88,
    89, 95, 110, 115
Osborn, Thomas Lee (T. L.), 90,
    99
Osterberg, Arthur, 26, 33
Ozman, Agnes, 23

Pacifism, Pentecostalism and: in
    WWI, 51–56; in WWII, 67–68
Palin, Sarah, 116–117
Palmer, Phoebe, 2, 5
Parham, Charles, 17, 22–28, 30,
    34, 35, 36, 38, 40, 45, 52, 83
Patriotism. See Nationalism
Patterson, J. O., 111, 120
Pentecostal acculturation: to
    evangelicalism, 68–69, 75,
    78–79, 106, 109, 142; to
    mainstream society, 62, 77,
    133, 134, 143–44
Pentecostal Assemblies of Jesus
    Christ, 64–65

Pentecostal Assemblies of the
    World, 46, 64–65, 100, 135
Pentecostal Bands of the World.
    See Nelson, Thomas
Pentecostal Church of God, 65,
    76, 99, 100, 122, 143
Pentecostal Fellowship of North
    America (PFNA), 69, 82, 111
Pentecostal Fire-Baptized
    Holiness Church, 44
Pentecostal Free Will Baptist
    Church, 34
Pentecostal Holiness Church,
    43, 44, 63, 69, 86, 100, 111, 134,
    143
Pentecostalism: African-American,
    43, 64–65, 100, 134; Holiness,
    42, 43–45, 63–64, 100, 133–34;
    Oneness, 42, 46, 64–65, 100,
    133, 134–35; Reformed, 42,
    45–46, 64, 65, 69, 100, 133
Pentecostalism, Jesus Name;
    Pentecostalism, Jesus Only. See
    Pentecostalism, Oneness
Pentecostalism, Wesleyan. See
    Pentecostalism, Holiness
Pentecostalism, Finished Word.
    See Pentecostalism, Reformed
Pentecostal-Roman Catholic
    Dialogue, 119
Pentecostal World Conference
    (PWC), 69, 77, 78, 82, 120
Pentecostal worship, 28–29, 60,
    94, 122
Perfectionism, 2, 13–15, 44,
    145
Phillips, William T., 46
Pietism, 3, 14, 57, 58
Pike, John M., 17, 25
Pinson, Mack M., 34, 37, 45
Piper, William Hamner, 34, 45

Pisgah Home and Gardens. *See* Yoakum, Finis

Politics, Pentecostalism and: apoliticism, 50–51, 108–9; political culture, 117–19; political progressives, 118; politicians, 108, 109, 111, 113, 115–17, 136n.1; politicization, 106–9, 112–17, 145; race, 106, 111–12

Popoff, Peter, 129

Positive confession, 85–86, 130–32

Pneumatology: in Holiness, 4, 15; in Pentecostalism, 28, 29, 38

Pragmatism, 16, 29, 62

Premillennialism, dispensational, 5–6, 8, 21, 50, 52, 53, 54, 70, 80, 119, 123, 145

Price, Charles S., 66, 79

Primitivism, 6, 8–9, 30–31, 38, 94, 96, 99

Professionalization. *See* Institutionalization

Progressive revelation, 6

Prosperity teaching, 81, 85, 87, 107, 126, 130. *See also* Positive confession

Protestant liberalism. *See* Protestant modernism.

Protestant modernism, 6, 57, 58, 59, 78

PTL Club, 115, 127–29, 130

Quakers, 5, 11, 13, 15, 22, 23, 35, 43, 52, 54

Race: and Holiness, 11–12; and Pentecostalism, 25, 26, 64–65, 66, 69, 100, 111, 134, 142–43, 145. *See also* Civil Rights, Pentecostalism and; Pentecostalism, African-American

Radical Holiness, 11–16; and gender, 12–13; and millenarianism, 21; and mysticism, 14; networks within, 16–18; and perfectionism, 13–14; pneumatology of, 15; and race, 12; and religious ecstasy, 11–12, 31; and social class, 11

Rapture. *See* Millenarianism

Rees, Seth Cook, 13, 16, 17

Religious Right, 106, 114–16, 118

Renewalists, 105, 141

Restorationism. *See* Primitivism

Revitalization movements, 79–80, 90, 91, 125–26

Rhema Ministerial Association International, 132

Richey, John R., 65

Rigorism, ethical. *See* Perfectionism

Roberts, Granville Oral, 83, 84, 86–90, 126–27, 130

Robertson, Albert, 113

Robertson, Marion Gordon ("Pat"), 91, 95, 114, 115, 116, 120, 121, 127

Robinson, Ida, 64, 67

Rodgers, H. G., 34, 45

Sanctification, 2, 4–5, 13–14, 24, 45; controversy over, 39–40

Sandford, Frank, 14, 17, 18, 21, 22, 23, 43, 84

Schleiermacher, Friedrich, 14, 57, 58

Second blessing. *See* Sanctification

Second Coming. *See* Millenarianism

Seed faith. *See* Prosperity teaching

Separation from the world, 49–51, 109, 134

Serpent-handling, 45, 77, 110

Seymour, William, 17, 25–28, 29, 35, 37, 39, 40, 41

Shakarian, Demos, 90, 119

Sharpton, Al, 116

Shouting. *See* Ecstasy, religious

Signs and wonders. *See* Supernaturalism.

Simpson, Albert Benjamin, 4, 7, 17, 23, 31, 36, 61

Sinclair, John Chalmers, 46, 65

The Sixties, 74, 86, 96–99, 101, 105, 106, 112, 113, 130

Slain in the Spirit. *See* Ecstasy, religious

Smale, Joseph, 25, 33

Smith, Charles ("Chuck"), 98, 121, 122

Smith, Hannah Whitall, 5

Smith, Mable, 67

Social class, 9, 10, 11–12, 50, 59, 94, 95

Southern Bible College, 122

Speckled bird theology, 66

Spiritual Warfare, 22, 80–81, 83, 87, 94

Spurling, Richard G., Jr., 41, 43

Stone, Jean. *See* Willans, Jean Stone

The Stone Church. *See* Piper, William Hamner

Supernaturalism, 6, 7, 15, 16, 17, 22, 45, 74, 79, 94, 99, 101; in deliverance movement, 81, 82, 85, 86, 88

Swaggart, Jimmy, 89, 115, 126–29, 131

Taylor, George Floyd, 34, 37, 44

Technological modernism. *See* Modernity, Pentecostalism and

Teen Challenge, 98

Televangelism, 88–90, 114–15, 126–29

Terry, Nealy, 26

Third wave of renewal, 105, 121

Tilton, Robert, 129, 131

Tomlinson, Ambrose Jessup, 17, 31, 34, 37, 41, 43, 45, 46, 50–51, 62, 63, 66, 108

Tongues, interpretation of, 28, 29

Tongues, speaking in. *See* Glossolalia

The Toronto Blessing, 125

Torrey, Reuben Archer, 4, 33

Trask, Thomas, 118, 132, 144

Trinity Broadcasting Network (TBN), 115, 124, 127, 129, 131

United Holy Church of America, 44, 64, 111

United Pentecostal Church, International, 65, 77, 100, 134, 135

Urshan, Andrew, 35, 41

The Vineyard, 121–23

Voice of Healing, 83, 88

Wacker, Grant, 58, 62, 144

Waggoner, Bert, 122–23

Warner, Daniel, 10, 17, 25

Washington for Jesus Rally, 115

Watson, George, 14

Watt, James, 115

Way of Faith, 17, 25

Welsh revival, 24, 25, 29

Wesleyan Methodist Church, 3, 10
White, Alma, 13, 17, 33, 37
Wigglesworth, Smith, 46, 79
Wilkerson, David, 93, 98, 99
Willans, Jean Stone, 92, 95
Williams, Smallwood, 100, 110
Women: in Holiness, 12–13; in Pentecostalism, 60, 64, 67, 142
Woodworth-Etter, Maria, 7, 12, 40, 46, 81
Word of faith. *See* Positive Confession

World Pentecostal Conference. See Pentecostal World Conference

Xenolalia, 23, 28. *See also* Glossolalia

Yoakum, Finis, 36, 83

Zimmerman, Thomas, 76, 78, 113, 116, 120, 132
Zion, Illinois, 17, 21, 22, 23, 25, 27, 34, 35, 83

About the Author

ROGER G. ROBINS is a Fulbright scholar and associate professor with specialization in American Studies at the University of Tokyo in Tokyo, Japan. Dr. Robins's previous works include *A. J. Tomlinson: Plainfolk Modernist*. He is the son of a Pentecostal minister.